THE MOVE METHODOLOGY

THE MISSING MANUAL FOR CRM

move
your customer
www.moveyourcustomer.com

Scan to access your free resource hub that includes bonus content, videos, templates, and articles.

https://link.moveyourcustomer.com/tmm

For further information, contact us at www.moveyourcustomer.com

ISBN: 978-1-923277-43-4 (paperback)

Printed in Australia by InHouse Print & Design.

InHouse PTY LTD Publishing

National Library of Australia

A catalogue record for this book is available from the National Library of Australia

TABLE OF CONTENTS

FOREWORD

CRM revolutionises businesses when implemented effectively.

With a single view of the customer, real-time performance metrics, streamlined processes, and teams taking ownership, CRM has the potential to transform the way you do business and provide exceptional customer experiences.

However, many CRM platform implementations fail to meet basic business expectations. They often appear too complex and do not deliver the expected value. They can be expensive to implement and end up being under-utilised.

That's because CRM is a strategic approach. It's the process of Customer Relationship Management. The real challenge is having the right skills and knowledge to create a simple and effective CRM strategy. It's crucial for business leaders to understand what CRM can do and how to design a strategy that benefits your customer and your business.

The 'MOVE' methodology focuses on filling this gap. Our goal is to provide you with the knowledge and tools to design a CRM strategy that's straightforward and impactful. We aim to equip leaders, managers, and functional teams with the language and approach needed to communicate effectively with technical teams to implement your strategy.

This book also provides technical teams with an understanding of what the business needs are and how to gather requirements in a way that makes sense. It really is the missing manual for CRM.

Who Are We?

Like many great relationships, we met at work! We have a shared passion for CRM and our skills, knowledge, and experience spanned the entire discipline. From strategy and planning to operations and technology, we understood the importance of the role each person played in the process.

Ian Sampson B. Comm. CA (SA)

A seasoned professional with a rich history in technology and business, Ian started his career as a Chartered Accountant with Ernst & Young, but his expertise has always revolved around the practical application of cutting-edge technology to improve businesses. This passion has led him to work for some of the world's largest companies across the UK, Europe, USA, Channel Islands, Africa, and Australia.

Kristen Makin: B. Comm. CSU (AUS)

A CRM and VIP marketing expert, Kristen's journey began in Europe in the online gaming industry during the early 2000s, where she had the privilege of working with some of the most innovative developers in the world. Throughout her career, she has successfully managed high value customers and teams, taking responsibility for them on an international scale.

Fiona Nilsson: B. Business. CSU (AUS)

An experienced Senior Marketing Executive who has worked with customer-centric companies spanning Australia, New Zealand, Europe, Asia, the UK, Ireland, and the USA. Fiona is passionate about the data and customer insights needed to make pragmatic business decisions within a marketing framework.

INTRODUCTION

This book was originally written for business leaders responsible for business growth who wanted to get the most out of their CRM investment.

However, through the writing process, we realised that while leadership support is vital to the success of customer relationship management and the implementation of CRM tools, business leaders simply can't be across all aspects and details of CRM.

There are teams of people connected to customer success and customer functions. In large organisations, you will find a CRM team responsible for the customer, while in small to medium businesses, the customer may bounce between departments, including sales, marketing, customer service, and operations. And let's not forget our technical teams and the important role they play in supporting CRM strategies through the enablement and management of software, platforms, and tools.

So, if you're a leader, manager, CRM specialist, in technical support, or have any other role with a connection to your customers, this book is for you.

It's our goal to help you understand what's important, why it's important, and explain everything you need to know but are too afraid to ask!

But how do you execute your CRM strategy on a platform and ensure a return on investment? How can you be confident in your ability to get the most out of the platform and lead your team effectively? How do you explain your business processes in a way that technical consultants can translate into a workable solution?

The success of any CRM implementation is determined by the detail in your CRM strategy.

As individuals, we have been involved in all types of businesses, from FTSE 500 companies to small and medium-sized businesses, since the early 2000s. Combined, we have over 60 years of experience in Information Technology (IT), Operations, Marketing, and Customer Strategy, where we have built and led CRM teams and implemented a range of CRM tools and platforms.

Over time, we have used many approaches to adapt to the evolving technology landscape. So, we combined our knowledge and experience to develop the MOVE methodology—designed to help businesses simplify their CRM strategy using straightforward methodologies and frameworks.

The Harsh Truth

According to a study by Salesforce, 50-70% of CRM implementations fail for the following main reasons

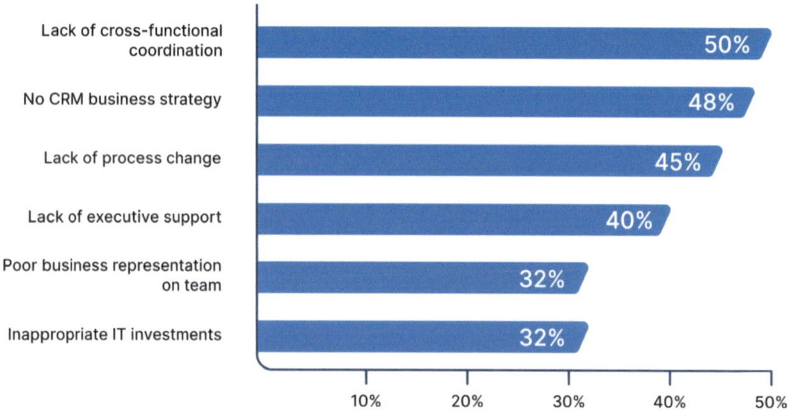

The perception is that most CRM implementations fail, but that's not the reality. It's very rare for CRM implementations to have a total technical failure. Rather, CRM platforms are often perceived as:

- Under-utilised
- Too complex

- Too expensive to implement
- Delivery time was longer than expected
- They aren't delivering the value that was expected
- Difficult to maintain

Take Control

The problem in the software industry is that most software vendors are focused on sales and selling a vision. They may sell you a solution, but they are not responsible for how well you use the software or the results you achieve, and they certainly don't help you define your CRM strategy.

When it comes to implementing software, most software companies rely on an ecosystem of implementation partners. Partners come with various levels of technical and implementation experience but do not have the same deep understanding of your business as you do. Their main priority is to quickly implement the solution and to deliver what was agreed, which is not necessarily what you needed.

Ultimately, the platform's success and the results the business delivers rest on your shoulders. You are accountable for driving the desired outcomes and maximising your CRM potential.

So, if over 50% of CRM implementations fail, what can be done to ensure you will be in the 50% that succeed?

We've found there is usually one of three key reasons for an underwhelming implementation:

- The initial planning was not sufficient
- There was a lack of engagement or ownership
- The ability to translate business requirements into technical solutions missed the mark

Software companies sell solutions. They don't implement them.

We wrote this book because there is no instruction manual that teaches the foundations of CRM strategy and how to relate it to the overall business.

OUT OF ORDER

THE SYSTEM WAS NEVER BROKEN, IT WAS BUILT THIS WAY

The MOVE methodology was developed to provide a step-by-step framework to effectively implement your CRM strategy on a CRM platform.

CRM platforms can deliver the promised results when everyone speaks the same language and can clearly articulate their needs from various perspectives (managers, administrators, partners, or account executives), adhering to a simple and common framework. However, the business must have a clear vision of how they want to manage their customer relationships, and the best way to approach this is to align your thinking to the customer lifecycle.

Customer Lifecycle is KING!

CRM is not a technology, it's a strategy and is best articulated using the principles of the customer lifecycle.

Defining your customer lifecycle helps businesses understand, monitor, and evaluate the stages customers pass through from initial awareness to disengagement.

Aligning your strategy with these stages clarifies your purpose, keeps customers progressing, and defines measurable outcomes, ensuring clear ownership and accountability throughout the customer journey.

Focusing on specific lifecycle phases allows you to prioritise challenges while maintaining alignment with your overarching strategy.

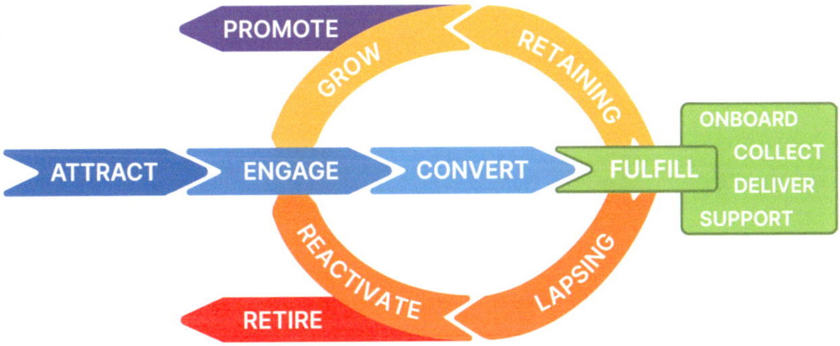

The MOVE Customer Lifecycle

Understanding the customer lifecycle is crucial for several reasons:

- **Tailored Communication:** Different stages demand different messages. Matching your communication to each phase ensures relevance and timeliness, whether educating during awareness or rewarding loyalty during retention.
- **Enhanced Customer Experience:** A well-crafted CRM strategy rooted in the customer lifecycle delivers personalised experiences at every touchpoint. Analysing behaviour allows proactive solutions, boosting overall satisfaction.
- **Increased Retention and Loyalty:** Active lifecycle management identifies engagement opportunities and resolves issues promptly, fostering stronger relationships and loyalty. Loyal customers are key to sustained profitability.

- **Resource Optimisation:** Segmenting customers by lifecycle stage enables efficient resource allocation. For example, prioritising high-value customers who are at risk of churning can yield better results than a blanketed approach.
- **Informed Decision Making:** CRM platforms yield rich customer data. Analysing this data within the lifecycle context provides insights into trends, preferences, and pain points, guiding data-driven decisions and continual strategy optimisation.

In essence, the customer lifecycle isn't just a concept—it's the backbone of CRM strategy, driving tailored communication, seamless experiences, and sustainable customer relationships.

How This Book Will Help You

You will gain:

- Control: of your processes
- Clarity: to see what's happening
- Confidence: to know what you must do next to make decisions
- Capability: to execute your plans and deliver the desired outcomes

This book takes you through the principles of CRM strategy and introduces an effective four-step approach called the MOVE methodology to enable you to clearly articulate your requirements in a way that technical teams can understand.

1. CRM Strategy

The most effective way to conceptualise your CRM strategy is to think about your customer's lifecycle and the journey they will be going on with you.

Highly successful adopters of CRM have achieved extraordinary results because they have put the customer at the centre of everything they do. Thus, they are truly customer centric.

Customer-centric thinking will enhance your understanding and utilisation of the frameworks we introduce later in the book.

2. The MOVE Methodology

MOVE is an acronym for the four principles you need to adopt to design a CRM strategy for implementation on your CRM platform.

The MOVE methodology emphasises the importance of defining customer and product journeys, processes across products and teams, and KPIs for measuring customer and business success.

The four principles are:

Map your journeys: This step guides you in mapping customer and product journeys, defining a high-level 'hero' customer journey and detailing your product paths.

Ownership: Clearly define the roles every person in your company has with respect to ensuring customer success. Each department is responsible for its processes, and everyone is accountable for transforming the business into a customer-focused organisation.

Visibility: Gain clarity on where each customer is on their journey with you. Obtain visibility into the performance of the company, the company managers, teams, and individuals, and measure the performance of processes to identify areas of optimisation.

Evolution: Foster an evolutionary approach rather than a revolutionary approach. Set up your business and CRM platform to continue evolving alongside your growth.

You will see the use of these MOVE symbols throughout the book. These have been designed to highlight the information that will be referred to when completing the MOVE templates and frameworks.

WHAT IS CRM?

Customer Relationship Management (CRM) is the strategic approach to maximising the value of your customers by knowing who they are and understanding their current stage within the customer lifecycle.

It's a set of practices aimed at nurturing and maintaining customer relationships to improve customer satisfaction, increase customer retention, and drive business growth.

CRM is a strategy, not a platform.

CRM is not just for sales and marketing; it is a priority for everyone in the business, from finance through to product delivery.

"One customer well taken care of could be more valuable than $10,000 worth of advertising."
– Jim Rohn

Why Strategy Matters

It's important to clearly identify your company's purpose, vision, mission, and values, and understand how they extend to your CRM strategy.

While your purpose is a statement that explains why you exist, your values dictate how you behave and treat each other. Values are not just important for building a strong and cohesive company culture, but they are also a powerful tool for attracting and retaining customers.

In simple terms, a strategy is a plan. If you define your CRM strategy aligned to the customer lifecycle, this essentially becomes the map of how you want your customers to interact with you. It represents the path you guide your customers on throughout their journey with you. If you execute this plan properly, you will have a unified view of the customer. This will help you understand their stage in the lifecycle at any given point and enable you to proactively guide them to their next best step or action.

Your strategy drives and defines how to maximise customer engagement (internal) and the customer experience (external) throughout the customer lifecycle.

To achieve a positive customer experience, you need a clear vision of how you want your customers to perceive your product or service. This enables you to gather relevant data points and measure your approach, allowing you to refine and optimise to enhance your customers' overall experience.

A well-executed CRM strategy has many benefits:

- **Customer Satisfaction and Retention:** CRM aims to improve customer satisfaction by understanding and meeting customer needs, providing exceptional service and addressing customer concerns. Businesses can increase customer loyalty and retention by building strong relationships and delivering value.
- **Sales and Revenue Growth:** CRM strategies and tools help optimise sales processes, manage leads and opportunities, and track customer interactions. This results in increased effectiveness within sales teams, revenue growth, and improved conversion rates.
- **Business Process Streamlining:** CRM enables businesses to streamline their processes by automating repetitive tasks, eliminating inefficiencies, and improving collaboration across teams. This enhances productivity and allows employees to focus on more valuable activities.
- **Customer-Centric Culture:** CRM fosters a customer-centric culture where everyone in the organisation recognises

the importance of customers and their needs. This culture influences leadership behaviours, system design, and decision-making processes to prioritise customer satisfaction and long-term relationships.

- **Customer Journey and Relationship Management:** CRM focuses on understanding the customer journey and managing customer relationships throughout the entire lifecycle. It involves collecting and utilising customer data to personalise interactions, anticipate needs, and provide tailored experiences.
- **Performance Measurement and Analysis:** CRM uses various metrics and analytics to measure and manage customer interactions and outcomes. This includes tracking customer satisfaction, customer lifetime value, sales performance, and other key performance indicators to identify areas for improvement and inform strategic decisions.
- **Team alignment:** CRM strategy defined in consultation with the marketing team, sales team, customer support team, and any other niche team ensures everyone is aligned and knows their roles, responsibilities, and handover points.

To be customer-centric, you need a strategy to achieve your goals. Without one, how will your technical team know the outcomes you need when implementing your platform? Without a clear plan and deliverables, they cannot build a solution.

It's not only about documenting your business processes. It's about seeing the big picture when defining your key customer journeys and the key milestones along that journey.

Leveraging CRM

A properly implemented CRM strategy enables you to leverage higher-level marketing initiatives and smart technologies that boost your customer engagement.

These include:

- **Customer Segmentation:** Segmenting customers based on their behaviours, preferences, actions, and needs can help you tailor your engagement strategies to each group. This helps you identify which customers you are at risk of losing and helps to prioritise reactivation efforts.
- **Personalisation:** Personalising interactions with customers can help build stronger relationships and increase engagement. This can include targeted marketing campaigns, personalised recommendations, or customised product offerings. These can also be aligned to any customer profiles you may have developed.
- **Data Analytics:** Collecting and analysing data on customer behaviour can help you identify trends, insights, and opportunities for improvement. This can then inform your engagement strategies and optimise your customer experience. It may also assist with refinement of your acquisition audiences and optimise budget spend.
- **Communication Channels:** Offering multiple communication channels can encourage customers to engage with your business in ways that are most convenient for them. This can include email, social media, chatbots, SMS, notifications, or phone support.
- **Continuous Improvement:** Continuously monitoring and optimising your customer lifecycle management strategies is critical to long-term success. Regularly reviewing customer feedback, analysing data, and testing new strategies can help you stay ahead of the curve and improve customer satisfaction and retention.

By clearly defining your CRM strategy and capability before your initial implementation or existing platform optimisation, you will ensure you have designed and tracked key customer data points and are ready for your future phases of more advanced capabilities, such as the ones mentioned above. This will help you avoid unnecessary rework.

Keep referencing your strategy when it comes to considering what data inputs and outputs you need to track and measure in order to review and optimise each stage of the customer journey.

YOUR PRODUCTS

A product is anything you agree to provide in exchange for something of value from your customer. Products can also be services; they don't have to be physical goods.

Products are all the touchpoints you offer, not just what you sell. A free eBook can be a 'product'. Whilst it has no price, a customer agrees to opt-in to your marketing and give you their contact details in exchange for free information.

In general, products have three core elements:

1. Agreement

There will usually be some type of agreement between you and your customer. This could be as formal as a signed contract for the sale of a high-value item, like a house. But it can be as informal as signed consent for something like a newsletter. E.g. you agree to deliver interesting information to your customer weekly, and in return, they consent to you having their contact details and having the right to communicate with them.

You can enter into these agreements at any time throughout the customer lifecycle; they can start early on in your marketing efforts, moving all the way through to upselling and cross-selling to existing customers.

2. Something You Will Provide

When you enter into an agreement, you have to deliver the customer the promised goods, services, or information that you said you would.

You need to record and track what has been ordered (or agreed) and what has been delivered, and this can give you valuable insights into what a customer is interested in, both now and potentially in the future.

The things you provide can be:

- Physical goods
- Services
- Intangible information
- Subscriptions or memberships
- Access to people or communities
- eBooks, newsletters, or lead magnets

3. Something They Give You in Exchange

There is always an exchange of value. Most often it is money, but it can be in return for other things of value, like information and the ability to communicate with a customer. This may well be the first time a customer has had a one-on-one interaction with you, whether it's with a salesperson or simply filling out an online form.

Purpose, values, and defining your products are all part of the MOVE methodology. Every step you and/or the customer take should align with your purpose and values. Defining your product types changes the way you think. While each product may be unique, the process and customer journey can be aligned by product type. This provides scalable, repeatable processes, resulting in your customers knowing what to expect and how to keep moving.

Who is Your Product For?

Your product will not be for everyone, so start thinking about who it's most suited to. For every product you offer, you need to know who the ideal customer is—it could be an individual or a company.

Personas and Segmentation

It's important for you to define not only who your customers are, but also what type of customers you want.

The process of creating a customer persona, also referred to as an avatar, will help clearly define your customers' needs and wants.

Consider the following:

- What is their buying pattern?
- What and where do they buy?
- What are their motivations for buying?
- What are their key demographics?

For example: 'Male millennials who have iPhones'

Thinking about personas will not only help you start to understand what customer data you need to track, but it will also define the audiences you want to target. Developing a customer persona can help you better understand your target audience and create more effective marketing and sales strategies.

Once you have your customer personas, you can be more targeted in creating acquisition audiences. You can start targeting audiences who you believe will align with your purpose and product offering.

When prospects start pouring in, how can you further qualify them so that you can focus on those who have a higher propensity to buy from you? Defining personas helps you create your qualifying questions.

What Are Qualifying Questions?

You need to qualify your prospects to see whether they actually need or want you and, more importantly, if you want them.

While you may have crafted a strong customer persona to determine who to market to, qualifying questions are an essential stage at the front end of a customer's journey. They help you to filter out prospects who may not be the ideal customer for you.

Qualifying your prospects is usually done by asking them a few key questions or creating a strong 'call to action' that measures their engagement and/or interest in your offering.

For each of your products, what are the questions you would ask your customer to determine if they really need your products? If their answer fits your criteria, they are your ideal customer.

Why Are Qualification Questions Important?

One of the objectives of CRM is to determine which clients are the most likely to benefit from you spending your very valuable time and resources:

With the right questions, you can:

- Optimise your marketing spend
- Learn more about your target audience
- Personalise the data you receive and store
- Better understand what solutions customers are looking for in their business
- Find out which lead responses best fit your business
- Determine which leads fit the company's persona description

All this valuable data helps your customer-centric business provide better solutions for your customers.

Your Product Purpose

Your products should align with both your purpose and how they solve problems for specific customers.

You might have several different products you sell, all aligned to the same purpose, but they are used to upsell or cross-sell opportunities into other products. Even a pre-sale download is a product. The steps your customer needs to take, and their expected outcomes need to be documented and measured.

You will need to start thinking about how to categorise your products into types. For example, you may have PDFs, webinars, and events as part of your offering.

The content of these may be different, and they may target different personas; however, the process that you define will be the same for each distinct product type.

You will use these categories when you start documenting your product journeys in the later chapters of this book.

Let's recap:

- You have a purpose
- Your products exist to achieve your purpose
- Every product solves a problem
- Not every person has the problem your product solves
- Identify the people who have the problem that your product solves
- Engage with and qualify those people
- Help those people move through your customer lifecycle

If you do all this, you will have happy customers who continue to buy from you and promote you.

These core principles lay the foundation for mapping your product and customer journeys. You will continue to anchor back to these when completing the MOVE methodology templates.

Document Your Products

You need to document your products. Remembering, products are all the touchpoints you offer, not just what you sell. Product types are a good way to refer to this.

- What type of product are you offering? Is it a meeting, event, content, or physical product?
- What is the objective of this product? Is it for engagement or revenue?
- Who is it targeting? Is it a new or existing customer?
- What are the metrics that matter for each product? The number of products sold? The number of email addresses? Or the number of meetings held?

By categorising products into core types, you create standardised and repeatable processes, leading to a more systemised approach that can be duplicated for future use.

> *Simplicity and scalability are the keys to growth in any business, and having standardised processes across products is crucial for achieving this.*

The Product Matrix

Managing and documenting all the products or touchpoints for a business can be a complex and overwhelming task. That's where creating a product matrix comes in handy. It is a strategic and organised approach that categorises your products into types, helping you understand their objectives and design scalable and reusable processes. By doing this, you gain insight into the role each product plays in your customer's journey.

Standardising and scaling your CRM processes becomes easier with this process.

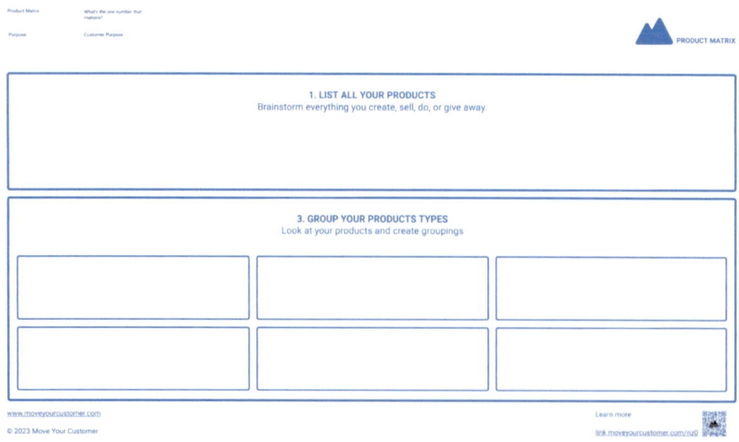

Product Matrix

Identify the Product Name:

Start by listing each product or touchpoint, such as events, content, webinars, or specific products like eBooks. Clear naming is key for easy identification.

Group by Product Type:

Organise products into categories (e.g., all events under 'Event'). This categorisation creates standardised processes for similar products, making your approach systematic.

The Power of Categorisation

It's vital to avoid reinventing the wheel with every new product development. Instead, embrace categorisation and identify core product types.

This approach allows you to standardise your journeys, making them repeatable and scalable. Trust us; this will be a game-changer for your business. Remember, not every product needs a unique journey. By grouping products into core types, you'll be able to design processes that work across all of them.

The Product Template

For each of the products (or product category) identified, we need to document their purpose and when to use them.

Define the Purpose:

State the purpose of each product. Whether it's to attract new customers, engage existing customers, or generate revenue, knowing the objective helps align your strategies effectively.

Set the Primary Objective:

Clarify if the main goal is attraction, engagement, or revenue generation. This guides your marketing strategies to meet specific goals.

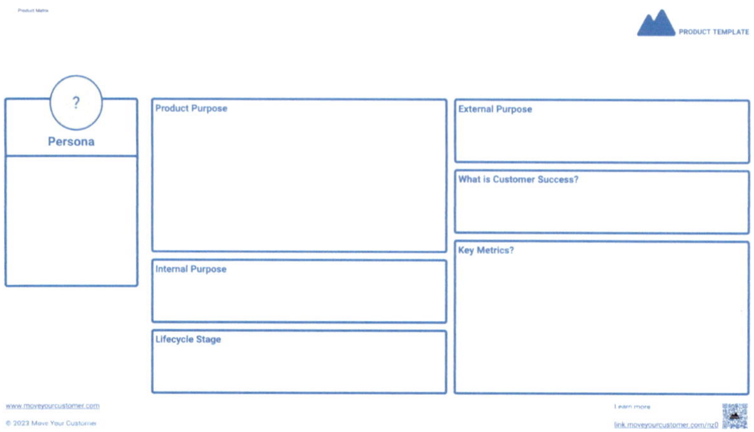

Product Template

Identify the Target Audience:

Determine who each product targets (new or existing customers). Tailor products to meet the needs and preferences of these specific groups.

Determine Relevant Metrics:

Choose metrics to measure each product's success, like sales numbers, engagement rates, or customer retention. These metrics offer valuable performance insights.

Understand the Customer Lifecycle Stage:

Document which stage of the customer lifecycle each product addresses. Aligning products with the customer's journey enhances their effectiveness.

The Hero Journey

If you offer multiple products, and you are upselling, cross-selling, or down-selling, you will need to map out your 'hero journey'.

Your hero journey aligns multiple products to your purpose, vision, and key lifecycle stages; it helps to connect customer journey maps with strategic objectives and measures progress.

By aligning your customer's journey through your products to deliver on your company's purpose, you create a seamless, consistent customer experience.

The hero journey may be redundant in some companies where there is only one product. In this case, you would only map out your product journey for that product.

Some companies may have more than one hero journey if they have two or more different customer segments looking to achieve different goals. This often happens in marketplace or broker industries, where your company is effectively matching buyers with sellers. You will have a hero journey for your buyers and a hero journey for your sellers.

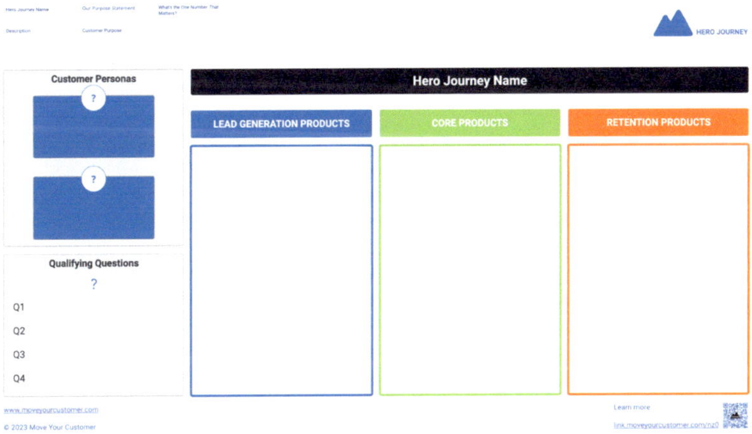

Hero Journey

CUSTOMER FUNDAMENTALS

In order to effectively optimise CRM and enhance customer relationships, it is crucial to understand the key terminology related to customers.

By familiarising yourself with the stages and identities of customers and how they align with your customer lifecycle, you can gain more clarity on how your customers are progressing.

When you establish a foundation for effectively tracking and managing customer interactions, you ensure that everyone within your business speaks the same language when it comes to understanding and discussing customers.

This knowledge enables you to identify opportunities for improvement, enhance customer satisfaction, and drive long-term outcomes.

Remember, by speaking the same language and having a unified understanding of customer terminology, you create a cohesive environment that fosters collaboration and customer-centricity throughout your organisation.

What is a Customer?

The word customer is very generic and can mean different things to different people. Is a customer someone you are trying to sell to? Or is a customer someone you have actually done business with?

When we use the term 'customer', we generally mean someone who has purchased your product or services and with whom you maintain an ongoing relationship.

Individuals who have not yet made a purchase are not considered customers in the true sense of the word.

Similarly, once customers have completed their payment and support contract, and they have moved on, they should not still be classified as a customer.

The Stages of Customer Identity

The term 'customer identity' refers to the different stages in the customer journey, where a customer can be identified and categorised based on their level of engagement and their readiness to buy.

By aligning customer identities with your key customer lifecycle stages, you can effectively map out the customer journey and design strategies to optimise each stage.

This alignment ensures that your efforts are focused on meeting customers' needs and expectations at every step, increasing their likelihood of conversion and long-term satisfaction.

The diagram below explains the different stages of customer identities—from being a member of an audience to a customer, through to a promoter or loyal customer. Some of your KPIs will be based on these customer stages and identities, so it's important to define them upfront.

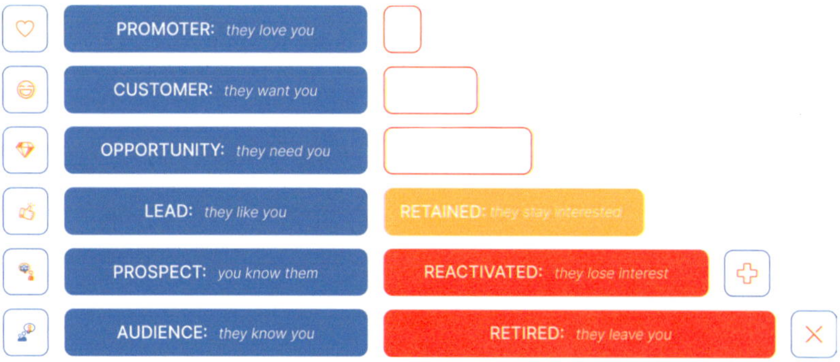

Stages of Customer Identity

Customer Identities

An Audience Member

They know you. But you don't know them. They may see you on social media, visit your stand at an expo, see an advertisement, or find out about you from a colleague or friend. Whilst you do not know them, you may know about them. Social media and advertising platforms will provide feedback on demographic information about the types of people who are engaging with you. You can use this data to refine your campaigns.

A Prospect

You know them. They have signed up for a newsletter or piece of content, scanned their pass at a conference, or left their business card. You have their basic details (name, email, phone number). You still have a lot of work to do to determine if they need or want you. If your marketing team believes there is an opportunity to make a sale, then they become 'marketing qualified' (MQL) and become a 'lead'.

A Lead

You know they like you. They have engaged with you over multiple touchpoints. We can measure this level of engagement by tracking the actions they take. They have downloaded your content, read your email, attended your free event, or followed your social channels.

> When you exhibit at a conference and scan all the badges of people walking past your stand, the details you gather are your prospects. However, you have very little idea if they are genuinely interested in you or not. You still have to go through all of these contacts and work out if they are worth pursuing. If they are, they become marketing qualified (MQL) and are a lead.

If you speak to the contact and they answer your qualifying questions favourably (like their budget, industry, and needs), then the contact is sales qualified (SQL) and should become an opportunity.

An Opportunity

They need you—they have answered your qualifying questions and are worthy of a conversation with a salesperson. The sales team focuses on converting opportunities into a sale. Once this happens, they become a customer.

People who become leads and opportunities and who don't buy from you become prospects again. However, it is important to remember them and segment them accordingly.

A Customer

They want you—they are an active customer who has bought your product or service, and they still have a relationship with you. They may still be paying you, or you might still be delivering their product or service, or providing support.

They will stay an active customer as long as you continue to support them, upsell, and cross-sell to them. When the relationship ends, they become an inactive customer, and you need to work out what to do with them.

A Promoter

They love you. They make repeat purchases and refer others to you. They like you and are loyal to you.

If a customer or a promoter doesn't want or need you, and your contractual relationship is over, then it may be time to part ways. Hopefully, things stay amicable, but regardless, you don't want to keep contacting them when you know the relationship is over.

Lapsing

They lose interest: You need to pay attention to customers who start to become less active. If you can identify that a customer is lapsing or dropping in value early, you can take steps to re-engage or reactivate them. You need to define clear measurements of what this means for your organisation.

Retired

You lose them. If you no longer have any relationship with an inactive customer, i.e. they have lapsed and you have been unable to reactivate them, then you should consider whether you should retire them. This can mean taking them off your marketing lists or even adding them to your marketing suppression lists. By doing this, you won't waste your marketing dollars or risk your email deliverability reputation on people who don't or won't like you.

These definitions, aligned to the customer lifecycle, form the basis of the MOVE mapping templates. You will want visibility of each of these stages to track how your customer identities are moving through the lifecycle stages and what you want to do when a 'customer' falls within this definition.

Qualification

Qualification is the process of assessing leads and prospects to understand whether they could be a good fit for your product or service. If you take this customer down your path to buy this product, how likely is it that your product will solve their problem, and they will be satisfied?

What is a Marketing Qualified Lead (MQL)

An MQL is a potential lead who has shown some level of interest in a company's products or services through marketing efforts.

MQLs are typically identified by marketing teams based on certain behaviours or characteristics that indicate a likelihood of becoming a customer.

Some common criteria that can be used to identify an MQL include:

- **Engagement:** The potential lead has interacted with the company's marketing materials, for instance, by downloading a white paper, attending a webinar, or following the company on social media.
- **Fit:** The potential lead fits the company's target demographic or persona, for instance, by working in a certain industry or having a certain job title.
- **Timing:** The potential lead is likely to make a purchase soon based on their behaviour or other indicators.

Once a potential lead is identified as an MQL, the marketing team will typically pass them along to the sales team for further follow-up and qualification. The sales team will then try to determine if the MQL is truly interested in making a purchase and, if so, will continue to work with them to move them through the sales funnel.

MQLs represent potential leads who have shown interest in a company's offerings and are, therefore, more likely to convert to paying customers with the right approach.

What is a Sales Qualified Lead (SQL)?

An SQL is a potential customer who has been identified by the sales team as having a higher likelihood of becoming a paying customer based on their behaviour and level of engagement with the company.

An SQL is typically identified by the sales team after an MQL has been passed to them by the marketing team. The sales team will then work to further qualify the lead and determine if they are truly interested in making a purchase.

Once a potential customer is identified as an SQL, the sales team will work to further nurture the relationship and move the lead through the sales funnel. This might include providing more detailed information about the company's offerings, addressing any concerns or objections the lead may have, and ultimately closing the sale.

SQLs represent potential customers who are highly likely to make a purchase, given the right approach. By identifying SQLs, the sales team can focus their efforts on those who are most likely to convert, which can lead to higher sales and revenue for the company. Qualifying questions in sales are those questions that help determine whether a lead meets the criteria defined in your strategy.

According to The Harvard Business Review, only 2-3% of leads will be ready to buy immediately. For some, you will need to have a series of conversations about the purchase, and the remainder will need to be sent to the lead nurturing pathway.

But don't worry, between 20-50% of potential clients will fall into the nurturing pipeline. As a rule, these leads often become your customers, providing a consistent, well-thought-out nurture sequence program is implemented. Reasons for not converting is often a great way to segment your customers and provide relevant information within your nurturing campaigns. This is often referred to as a closed/lost reason code.

One of our authors, Fiona, has an example of this:

> As a Marketing Director for a company selling business courses, I worked very closely with the sales team to monitor the leads pipeline. The majority of our leads came from paid campaigns on social media, so we could control the number of leads coming into the business. However, we were not always able to control the quality of the leads who booked appointments with a sales consultant. We introduced qualifying questions prior to the appointment booking, which

allowed us to redirect MQLs that would not qualify as SQLs to nurturing while only passing qualified leads to the sales consultants. We saw a 25% decrease in the volume of leads to the sales team, but a 40% increase in conversion rates to purchase because we could identify which customers were suitable and ready to buy.

ANUM: Authority, Need, Urgency, Money

You can categorise qualifying sales lead questions according to the **ANUM** sales process—Authority, Need, Urgency, and Money.

- **Authority:** Are you communicating with the right person? This contact may not be responsible for the company's final decision making regarding the purchase of the product/service. This is where you need to find out who makes the final decision and get that person's contact. Or, if more than one person makes the decision, contact all of them and talk to each of them.
- **Need:** Does your product/service solve your lead's problems? Learn more about your potential customer's business, research their industry, and learn about their pain points. That way, you can see if you'll be useful.
- **Urgency:** Find out what is going on in the lead's company. Perhaps the potential client's company is going through structural changes, considering transformation, or is actively recruiting. This additional data can help you learn more about how important it is for the lead to solve their issue. To put it simply, qualification helps your sales team prioritise where to focus their attention. Your most qualified leads have the biggest potential for being converted into paying customers.
- **Money:** With the help of sales qualifying questions, find out what the potential client's budget for the product is. This part of communication needs to be approached very carefully. Beforehand, you need to find out what products the lead is currently using, and what their ideal price range

is for similar solutions. You can also get a rough estimate of their budget by going into their business profile before you ask questions about their finances in person. If you establish a good connection with the lead at this point, you can now negotiate a deal.

Qualification helps your sales team prioritise where to focus their attention. Your most qualified leads have the biggest potential for being converted into paying customers.

- **Shorten the Deal Cycle:** Sales teams can quickly identify potential buyers, not wasting time on prospects who have no intent to purchase.
- **Identify Product Needs:** Determine if the customer has a problem your product can solve.
- **Target the Right People:** Offer products to the decision makers to avoid wasting time.
- **Faster Customer Segmentation:** Build relationships and personalise communication for each segment.
- **Gain Long-Term Customers:** Focus on ready-to-buy leads, increasing chances for long-term customers.

All of these benefits will give you an increase in marketing and sales productivity, significant savings in time and money, and more opportunities to help your customers.

Some tips:

- Keep your qualifying questions limited to a maximum of five questions. The more questions you need your prospects to answer, the more prospects you will lose along the way.
- When asking qualifying questions, it's important to focus on the end goal of selling your ultimate product.
- It's important to make your qualifying questions quantifiable. Avoid asking open-ended, free-form questions. Open-ended responses present a challenge when it comes to automating follow-up actions in your CRM platform.
- Make answering qualifying questions mandatory but capture the customer profile and contact details first, then

ask the qualifying questions afterwards. If customers stall when completing them, you can reach out to them again.

"It takes months to find a customer, seconds to lose one."
– Vince Lombardi

Defining and measuring your MQL and SQL criteria gives you visibility of the metrics that matter and helps you refine and optimise your marketing strategies. For example, if your MQL conversion rate is below 50%, you can assess whether you need to increase your acquisition spend or refine your target audience.

Measuring Customer Engagement

In any journey, reaching the destination is critical; to get there, you must keep moving. Understanding and measuring velocity is key to achieving success and driving efficiency.

Velocity refers to the speed at which customers progress through the various stages of their journey within your product lifecycle.

Examples of Velocity

Acquisition Velocity: This measures how quickly your company attracts, engages with, and converts potential customers. Efficient tactics like targeted advertising, content marketing, and social media play pivotal roles in achieving high acquisition velocity.

Sales Velocity: This focuses on the speed at which leads become customers. Optimise by defining a streamlined sales process using automation, lead scoring, and timely follow-ups.

Retention Velocity: This gauges your ability to engage with and retain customers. Use personalised marketing, loyalty programs, targeted emails, and exceptional customer service for high retention velocity.

Service and Delivery Velocity: Measure the timeliness with which you deliver your products or services. Streamline supply chains, reduce delivery times, and provide excellent customer service.

Measuring Velocity: Track customer progression, identify areas for improvement, and align with customer-centric thinking for better experiences.

Grading and Ranking

Grading and ranking (or scoring) are handy tools within a CRM system to measure customer engagement. They help businesses efficiently manage interactions and prioritise leads or customers.

Grading involves assigning a specific score or grade to each lead or account, reflecting the level of interest a customer has in you. It is usually based on the actions a customer takes. This may be that they open an email, visit a web page, download a file, or attend a meeting. A higher-grade lead represents a more promising opportunity and thus receives increased attention from sales and marketing teams.

Ranking, on the other hand, involves sorting leads or accounts based on importance or priority. These scores are often calculated based on responses to your qualifying questions.

While this may not be a priority for you in the initial phase, it is important to think about how you will grade and rank customers in the future.

Why, you ask? Because you need to ensure you have captured the data points needed for ranking and grading to avoid duplicating work in future phases to add them. This is an extremely valuable capability for your marketing and sales teams as it allows them to prioritise contacts based on how the lead has been ranked.

The MOVE Engagement Matrix

The MOVE engagement matrix is a strategic tool designed to help you better segment and manage your customers by determining who benefits most from your time and resources. It operates on two axes: the vertical axis measures whether a customer needs you (sales qualified), and the horizontal axis measures whether they like you (marketing qualified). By analysing these dimensions, you can classify customers into four distinct quadrants, each requiring different approaches.

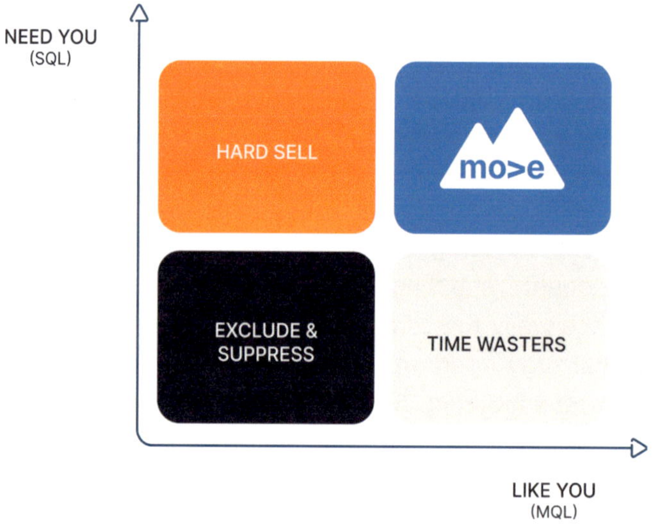

The MOVE Qualification Matrix

The 'MOVE' Quadrant

The top right 'MOVE' quadrant represents your ideal customer and is the focal point for designing all your CRM processes. Customers in this segment are both engaged and in need of your products and services. They are identified as marketing qualified by measuring their level of engagement and interest through their actions. They also need your offerings, as evidenced by their responses to your qualification questions. These questions might include profiling inquiries about their income, industry, years in business, and number of employees, which are determined when filling out your product templates and matrices.

You should design your processes with the top right quadrant in mind, as these are your ideal customers.

The 'Hard Sell' Quadrant

In the top left quadrant, customers need your services but are not yet engaged. This quadrant represents traditional sales efforts, often involving cold outreach, inside selling, and prospecting. While there's a clear opportunity based on the customer's need, you must work harder to build trust and engagement. These prospects may not know you, so your sales processes will be less efficient as you convince them to like and trust your brand. These customers are often put on nurturing journeys to 'warm' them up and give them more information, getting them ready for the sales team to re-engage.

The 'Time Wasters' Quadrant

The bottom right 'Time Wasters' quadrant includes customers who show high interest but are not a good fit for your product. These might be small companies or start-ups without the purchasing power, budget, authority, or alignment with your industry. Engaging with these prospects can drain your resources and time, as they may never buy or, worse, they could make a purchase that ends poorly. This can lead to reputational damage, necessitate refunds, and damage control.

As a business, you need to work out where to draw the line and how to identify which customers you want to help and those whom you can't.

The 'Exclude and Suppress' Quadrant

The bottom left quadrant is customers who neither need nor like your services. This group can include customers who are leaving, those who are a poor fit, or even competitors scoping out your offerings. It's crucial to disengage these individuals from your marketing and outreach activities to avoid negative interactions and protect your internal information.

By utilising the MOVE engagement matrix, you can strategically allocate your resources and efforts, ensuring that you focus on the right customers who will bring the most value to your business.

What's the Value of Your Customer?

Let's delve into the importance of measuring customer value and how it can significantly impact your organisation.

By gathering customer data from various touchpoints and consolidating it into your CRM platform, you can gain a comprehensive understanding of each customer's interactions with your business and their overall value to your organisation.

Customer data scattered across multiple sources can lead to a lack of understanding regarding the total value of your customer. As a result, you may unintentionally underrate certain customers who have generated substantial revenue over time.

Having a complete view of your customers' interactions enables you to identify which products or services they are willing to pay more for. This valuable insight will empower you to make better pricing decisions and maximise your revenue streams.

It also enables you to identify your most valuable clients and those at risk of leaving. By focusing on retaining high-value customers, you can improve customer retention and increase lifetime customer value. You can put pre-emptive strategies in place before customers leave.

Furthermore, a comprehensive view of your customers' interactions will allow you to pinpoint the products or services that most interest them, enabling you to tailor your marketing efforts accordingly. This targeted approach helps you to avoid wasting marketing spend on products or services that your customers are not interested in.

By understanding the true value of each customer, you can make more accurate sales forecasts and plan accordingly. This allows you to allocate resources more efficiently, ensuring your business operates more smoothly and profitably.

Remember, measuring customer value is not just about data collection; it's about gaining actionable insights about the value of your customers in order to make informed decisions for your organisation.

Customer Lifetime Value

An important customer measurement is lifetime value (LTV), which measures the total amount of revenue a customer is expected to generate over the course of their relationship with you.

Customer Lifetime Value Calculation

Customer Lifetime Value (CLV) is a metric that can help you achieve a balance between your short-term and long-term marketing goals. By understanding the financial return on your investments, you can make better decisions that lead to more profitable outcomes. With CLV, you can prioritise your efforts towards acquiring customers with a higher value, which results in spending less time and resources on those with lower value.

Customer Satisfaction and Feedback

"A satisfied customer is the best business strategy of all."
– Michael LeBoeuf

Customer satisfaction is just one measurement of customer experience.

Satisfied customers with a positive customer experience can also be an indication of the success of your CRM strategy. They can ultimately deliver ROI on your CRM platform implementation. They are proof that you are providing good experiences and are delivering value.

A universal engagement metric that is easy to implement and track is the customer's Net Promoter Score (NPS). NPS is a widely used market research metric based on a single survey question asking respondents to rate the likelihood that they would recommend a company, product, or service to a friend or colleague.

"If you make customers unhappy in the physical world, they might each tell six friends. If you make customers unhappy on the internet, they can each tell 6,000."
– Jeff Bezos

Calculate your NPS using the answer to a single question, 'How likely is it that you would recommend [brand] to a friend or colleague?' using a 0–10 scale

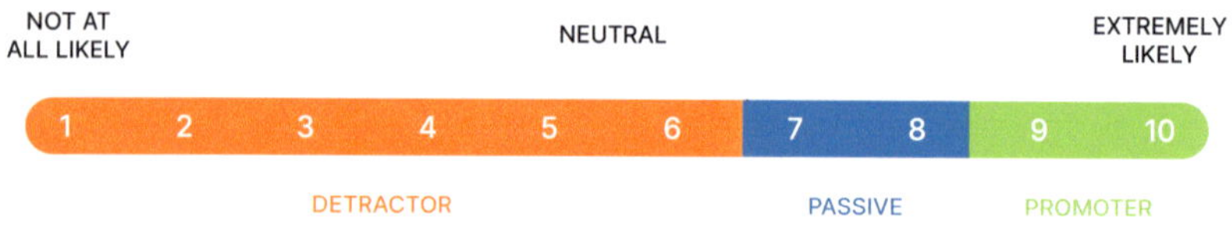

Promotors (%) less Detractors (%) = NPS

While this is the most common way that companies measure customer satisfaction, regular customer feedback and surveys are essential for understanding customer needs.

Feedback is a Gift

Feedback is a gift — it helps to drive continuous improvement, measure satisfaction and loyalty, identify risks, personalise experiences, foster engagement, enhance products and services, and build trust. By leveraging these insights at each stage of the customer lifecycle, you can optimise your CRM strategies and deliver better outcomes for your customers.

"We all need people who will give us feedback. That's how we improve." – Bill Gates

When you start mapping your customer journeys, clearly identify which stages you want to seek feedback. Feedback and surveys are key components of a great CRM strategy.

Measuring Return on Your CRM Platform Investment

Measuring the Return on Investment (ROI) for your CRM platform implementation is crucial to understanding its overall impact on your business goals, objectives, and efficiency. To effectively measure ROI, you need a structured approach that can be measured against your original business case for implementing the platform.

Here are some steps to help you measure your ROI effectively:

1. Define Clear Objectives

The first step in measuring ROI is defining specific and measurable objectives for your CRM implementation phase. Whether your focus is on boosting sales, reducing churn, or streamlining processes, clarity in your objectives is essential. These objectives will serve as the guiding stars to measure your CRM platform's success.

2. Identify Key Performance Indicators

Once you have defined your objectives, identify the Key Performance Indicators (KPIs) that align with them. For instance, if you are aiming to improve your sales pipeline, relevant KPIs might include sales conversion rates. Choose indicators that directly reflect the goals you want to achieve.

3. Set the Baseline

Before you launch your CRM platform, establish a baseline for the identified KPIs. This baseline provides a benchmark against which you can measure the impact of your CRM implementation. It also helps you to gauge the progress made over time.

4. Calculate the Value

To measure ROI, calculate the increase in KPIs from your baseline and compare them against the costs associated with your CRM platform implementation. Consider factors such as software licensing, implementation services, training, new hires, ongoing maintenance, and the required timeframe. This financial impact assessment will help you to understand the tangible benefits gained from your investment.

5. Consider Qualitative Factors Beyond The Numbers

Remember that ROI isn't just about dollars and cents. Consider qualitative factors like improved customer satisfaction, enhanced team collaboration, process efficiency, and visibility. These factors contribute to overall business success and should be part of your ROI evaluation.

6. Review and Refine

As your CRM implementation progresses, regularly review your metrics measurement and refine if necessary. Be open to making adjustments to your strategy based on insights gained from data analysis and feedback from users. Flexibility and adaptation will lead you to greater success.

7. Measure, Thrive, and Grow

Measuring the ROI of your CRM investment is not just a formality, it's a strategic imperative. By adopting a structured approach and considering both quantitative and qualitative factors, you'll not only measure success but you'll also uncover opportunities for continuous improvement and growth.

It is also vital to establish clear goals and objectives for the CRM platform implementation, such as increasing sales or improving customer service, and to regularly review progress towards these goals.

Finally, it is important to ensure that the CRM platform is being used effectively by all relevant teams and that data is being entered accurately and consistently because your CRM platform is only as accurate as the data you enter.

THE MOVE METHODOLOGY

MOVE
methodology

The MOVE methodology consists of four principles for designing a successful CRM strategy. M.O.V.E. is a simple acronym for Map, Ownership, Visibility, and Evolution.

The MOVE Methodology Defines the Four Principles of CRM Success

The MOVE methodology emphasises the importance of defining technology and customer roadmaps, customer and product journeys, processes across products and teams, and KPIs for measuring customer and business performance.

As we have explained, CRM strategy is most effectively defined when it is centred around the customer lifecycle.

This approach revolves around understanding, mapping, and tracking the various stages a customer goes through when interacting with your business. And how your relationship changes with your customer throughout that journey.

This methodology is the culmination of years of identifying and addressing common patterns in misaligned CRM strategies and CRM platform underutilisation.

Our objective is to equip you with the knowledge, tools, and confidence to define your CRM strategy clearly. This strategy should be easily understandable for everyone, from non-technical business leaders to CRM technical experts. When everyone speaks the same language, implementation projects are less likely to fail, thanks to the clarity and alignment in understanding goals, processes, and outcomes.

When everyone speaks the same language, implementation projects are less likely to fail, thanks to the clarity and alignment in understanding goals, processes, and outcomes.

The framework simplifies capturing and documenting the necessary steps to ensure every customer keeps progressing through the customer lifecycle. By aligning customer strategy, processes, and metrics, you will find it easier than ever to harness the full potential of your CRM system. This is not just about technology; it's about creating a unified approach that integrates business strategies with customer needs, ensuring a smooth and successful journey for both your business and your customers.

Let's run through each of these in turn:

M is for Map:

Map every step of your customer journey. This mapping exercise is broken down into four principles, and we give you the tools and templates to complete each layer.

O is for Ownership:

Assign Ownership to every facet of the customer journey. Clearly define the roles of every person in your company to ensure customer success. Each department is responsible for its processes, and everyone is accountable for transforming the business into a customer-focused organisation. A critical component of CRM is assigning internal ownership to every stage of every customer's journey. This level of ownership fosters a culture of accountability for business performance.

V is for Visibility:

Get visibility of the metrics of every step of your customer journey. Gain clarity into the performance of managers, teams, and individuals, as well as the company's overall performance. Then, measure where every customer is on their journey with you. You can make better decisions and constantly improve your processes with all this information.

E is Evolution:

CRM strategy implementation is a constant evolution, not a one-off project. Embrace continuous improvements. And set a pace of change that matches your capability, resources, and budget.

How did the MOVE methodology come about?

Ian, one of the co-authors of this book, explains how he started on this pathway to develop the MOVE methodology.

"In 2005, I co-founded a consultancy with a small, dynamic team scattered across the globe, building high-end, secure intranets for our enterprise clients. We were passionate about our work but lacked the tools to unleash our potential. That was until we stumbled upon Salesforce.

"We were clueless about sales processes and marketing strategies, but we knew we needed a way to keep track of our growing business opportunities. So, we took a leap of faith and implemented Salesforce, hoping for the best. That decision would be a game-changer for our company.

"The moment we gained visibility over our existing customers and their contracts was nothing short of a revelation. We realised we had been on the verge of dropping the ball on some of our most important service agreements. Suddenly, we could see the bigger picture, and it was electrifying.

"With Salesforce by our side, we accelerated the growth of our business at an astonishing pace. We transformed from a small, niche team into a force to be reckoned with in the corporate web services industry. The power of having all our clients and their opportunities at our fingertips was phenomenal.

"We now had a comprehensive view of our sales processes, allowing us to make informed decisions and take calculated actions. We became proactive in identifying potential issues and honouring our commitments to our clients. We were no longer just delivering projects; now, we were forging long-lasting relationships built on trust and reliability.

"Salesforce became our secret weapon, helping us streamline our operations and navigate the complex world of marketing. We may not have had prior knowledge or expertise, but Salesforce provided us with the tools and insights we needed to succeed. It empowered us to maximise our potential and exceed our expectations.

"Collaboration was key to our success. Salesforce became our virtual headquarters, connecting us seamlessly and providing real-time information. It fuelled our efficiency and allowed us to synchronise our efforts, resulting in flawless execution and exceptional client satisfaction."

M IS FOR MAP

MAP

In our experience, this mapping—or lack thereof—is where organisations start to stumble when implementing their CRM strategy on a CRM platform.

Without this critical step, teams often focus on short-term goals and fail to see the big picture, which can lead to long-term challenges and consequences.

Without a high-level map of the customer journey, teams tend to work in silos that create a fragmented customer experience. This lack of collaboration leads to confusion, frustration, duplication of effort, poor performance, and a poor customer experience.

For instance, when marketing launches a new campaign to sell a product, it's essential to brief the sales team properly. Without this, the sales team might not be prepared to handle customer inquiries or set appropriate expectations, leading to lower conversion rates. Similarly, if marketing introduces a new incentive program without adequately informing the accounts team, there could be a disconnect regarding discounts and special terms promised, causing customer confusion and dissatisfaction.

"If you fail to plan, you are planning to fail."
– Benjamin Franklin

To avoid such issues, businesses must take a holistic approach and consider the entire customer journey.

Why Don't We Plan?

In our fast-paced business world, where immediate results are highly prized, the idea of dedicating substantial time to planning can seem counterintuitive. Companies often prioritise short-term gain over long-term benefits, and ironically, running a planning workshop is seen as a roadblock to getting things done. But in reality, failing to plan creates more roadblocks in the future.

For many, the planning process can appear overwhelming; a lack of appropriate tools, knowledge, and expertise often compounds this uncertainty.

Without a clear plan and roadmap, organisations struggle to identify the most crucial aspects of their business to address first. Additionally, the perceived complexity of planning processes can deter efforts. When working with a sophisticated CRM system, the task of dissecting and understanding each component to create an effective plan can seem daunting, especially for those without technical expertise.

Overcoming these challenges requires a shift in perspective:

- View planning as an investment rather than a cost. Our methodology and templates substantially reduce the time you need to invest to capture your basic CRM strategy and processes.
- Adopt our tools, templates, and methodologies to design CRM strategies and processes to substantially improve the return on investment of your CRM implementation.

CUSTOMER LIFECYCLE, THE FOUNDATION OF CRM STRATEGY

The foundation of CRM strategy is the customer lifecycle. The key stages a customer goes through from the moment they first become aware of your business or product to the point where they no longer interact with it is called the customer lifecycle.

The problem with most customer lifecycle models is that they are very marketing centric. They often only focus on winning customers and don't go beyond the initial sale. They don't take into account the entire customer lifecycle.

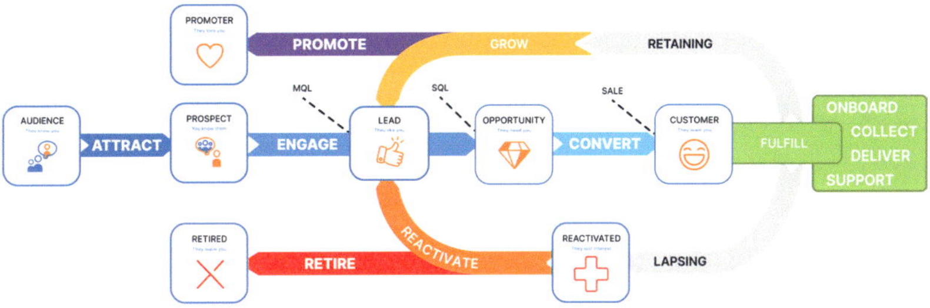

So, we developed a customer lifecycle that covers every stage of the customer's relationship with your business. It covers those critical stages beyond the sale, including how the sale is fulfilled through upsell and cross set, to the often-forgotten stage of retirement and how you gracefully offboard a customer.

The Key Customer Lifecycle Stages

The best way to start thinking about your CRM strategy is via the customer lifecycle. In many organisations, the different stages are often owned by different areas of the business; however, the information gained at each stage is often reused later in the customer journey.

By breaking it down, it becomes easier to articulate what you or the customer needs to do to keep moving through the stages, and what you need to measure along the way.

It also encourages ownership of each stage and promotes greater collaboration between departments.

Attract

The customer becomes aware of your business or product through various marketing channels, such as social media, search, advertisements, or word of mouth.

They are an audience member. You may know them, but they are unknown to you. If you are targeting specific marketing demographics, you may have information about their demographic.

Defining your customer personas helps you to establish your audience types for digital media. By ensuring you track your audience types, you can start measuring which audiences and content is the most successful in attracting the right leads that convert to sales.

Engage

The customer has shown some level of interest in your product or service. They may have visited your website, attended a demonstration, or expressed interest in a particular product or service. The customer is now considering whether or not to purchase your product or service.

Customers first enter the 'Engage' stage when they identify themselves with you, usually through a web form where they provide some information about themselves. At this point, they are considered a prospect until you can determine if they are genuinely interested in you.

You can measure their level of interest by the actions they have taken, such as website visits, downloads, calls answered, or meetings attended. Once their interest is validated through these actions, they become a lead.

Marketing Qualified Leads (MQLs): Leads where marketing believes there is an opportunity for a sale. This is usually determined from marketing data collected.

At this stage of the product journey, you should ask qualifying questions to determine if they are the right fit for your products. If they are, they should be converted into an opportunity.

Sales Qualified Leads (SQLs): Qualified by the sales team, usually from a direct call or conversation. The client passes the qualification questions, confirming their fit for the product.

Convert

The 'Convert' stage is your sales process, where you have the opportunity to persuade the customer, through a defined series of steps (your sales process), to purchase your products or services.

By defining clear steps within your convert stage, you can easily see where your leads are within this stage of the lifecycle. You could trigger off reminders or even generate lists for your sales team so they can keep moving the customer through to purchase. This is also a stage where you can create reasons for the sales not converting. Create a pick list of why the lead has not converted and, based on these reason codes, you can either remove the lead from your list, or re-nurture them based on the reason, warming them back up for the sale.

Fulfil

After a customer has made a purchase, it's crucial to fulfil your end of the contract. This includes getting the customer started with the product or service, delivering it, invoicing and collecting payments, and providing ongoing support.

Hence, the 'Fulfil' stage often consists of four sub-stages:

- **Onboard:** Make sure the customer is properly introduced to your product or service by providing the necessary training, resources, and information to get started.
- **Collect:** Send the invoice and collect the money owed, which may involve handling late payments, refunds, and bad debts.
- **Deliver:** Deliver the product or service, which involves the logistics and processes to get it to the customer.
- **Support:** Provide ongoing support for your customer with your product and service, including handling customer service inquiries, technical issues, repairs, and ensuring overall satisfaction.

Retain

After the customer has made a purchase, you retain their business by delivering and providing great customer service, ongoing communication, and support. Most importantly, keep renewing, upselling, and cross-selling to this customer group.

Retention marketing is the key to maximising customer value. Making sure you have the right data stored can help you communicate relevant information regarding your product and services, to keep the customer engaged. By tracking the products and services they are currently using, you can also see what other products and services they may be interested in and showcase new product releases.

For those not engaging actively in your product or service, you can create engaging content via email, SMS, or even outbound calling.

"Repeat customers spend 67% more than new customers" – BIA Advisory services

By having all your inbound and outbound communications stored in a centralised area, you can ensure you provide the best customer service. Your service team can quickly see all the communications between the customer and be able to have meaningful conversations.

Promote

You are turning your satisfied customers into influences and advocates. Encourage them to leave positive reviews, share their experiences with others, and refer new customers to your business.

How and when will you ask for customers to provide reviews? How will you monitor them? We all like to read reviews before we make a purchase. Make sure this is a key part of your CRM strategy. And more importantly, ensure you can identify advocates and work out ways to thank them for their loyalty.

Positive customer reviews and feedback as a core part of a customer strategy will provide independent validation of your product and services.

Lapsing

After a customer purchases your products but no longer engages with you, they are classified as 'lapsing'. Pay attention to this group and find ways to re-engage them to retain them as ongoing customers.

Define the metrics that matter for you to measure if a customer is becoming disengaged. Focus your marketing efforts on getting them back up to their previous behaviours. Consider what data you will need to do this.

Reactivate

When customers stop purchasing your products for a predefined period of time, they are considered inactive. You have an opportunity to reactivate these customers with new products and offers.

For those that have chosen to cancel or leave, create a survey to understand their reasons for leaving. This can be passed on to the product team and when this reason is addressed, it's a great way to reactivate your customer.

Retire

When customers stop using your product or service, or no longer align with your business, you need to gracefully offboard and exclude them from your active customer communications. This preserves your brand's reputation.

It's okay for a customer to leave you. The important thing is to ensure you offboard them respectfully, and you find out why they decided to leave. This information can be very useful for your product and operational teams to help them optimise the product and service offering. If they continue to consent to be contacted, segment them accordingly and only go back to them when you have addressed the reason they left.

Some customers you may not want, and that's okay, too. Just ensure that you suppress them and ensure you don't market to them or try and re-engage them later. It's okay not to want a customer if they don't align with your goals and purpose.

The Ultimate Customer Lifecycle Diagram

At this stage, you now know the language and principles of defining a customer lifecycle and the various. We can combine all of this into a single image.

- Lifecycle stages (attract, engage, convert, etc.)
- Customer identities (audiences, prospects, leads, etc.)
- Phases of a customer relationship (know, like, want, etc.)
- Qualifications (MQL, SQL)
- How and when to measure customer engagement

This is your customer lifecycle blueprint and the basis for the MOVE methodology and templates. Ensure you identify and

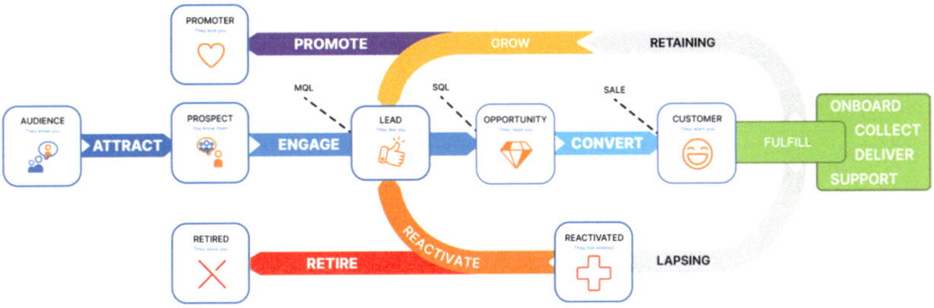

Customer Lifecycle, Relationships, and Identities

document at which stage you will enable your key questions and surveys to measure customer engagement.

Mapping the Customer Lifecycle

The stages of a customer relationship—from when a customer is part of an audience where they know you but you don't know them, to when they identify themselves to you—continues as they come to like you, need you, and want you, culminating in a sale and, ultimately, loving you and becoming promoters of your brand.

The stages in the customer lifecycle are crucial for transitioning customers through different points of the relationship. These stages are labelled as follows: attract, engage, convert, fulfil, retain, reactivate, retire, and promote. Each of these stages represents the activities WE need to perform to move our ideal customer, or customer persona, through THEIR lifecycle to and through our products.

Mapping out the customer lifecycle at a high level is useful, but the real work happens within each stage. Each stage of the lifecycle defines the specific processes and activities required to engage with our customers and keep them progressing through their lifecycle. By focusing on these stages, you ensure continuous engagement and satisfaction, ultimately leading to loyal customers who advocate for your brand.

We provide two templates to help you map out your CRM processes. The first is our product journey template. This template outlines the customer lifecycle for each product or product type. You should define the customer lifecycle for your ideal customers and map out how they progress through each stage of the lifecycle at a high level.

In this template, we detail the order in which activities need to be completed and identify who is responsible for each stage at a high level. It ensures that your whole team is aligned, and you deliver a consistent customer experience throughout the customer life cycle.

The second template we provide is called the MOVE canvas. This template dives into the details of each stage of the customer lifecycle. It clearly defines what your team needs to do at every stage to keep your customers progressing. The MOVE canvas becomes your requirements and definitions document, which you can hand over to your technical team. This documentation makes it easier for a technical team or CRM team to pick up and implement as part of your ongoing CRM evolution. By using this template, you ensure that your CRM processes are clearly defined, systematically organised, and continuously improved.

THE PRODUCT JOURNEY

For every product (or categories of similar products), you need to map out the lifecycle of the customer as they progress on their journey to, and through, that product. This product journey sets out the processes you need to implement to keep each customer moving forward. And for the milestones they should reach along the way, YOU need to start defining WHAT is required to keep each customer progressing on their journey with you.

Consider the following:

- A journey is comprised of the lifecycle stages
- Each stage is interconnected with other stages in the lifecycle
- The end of one stage marks the start of another
- Every stage is owned by one team, which is responsible for the outcomes of that stage
- Every stage of a journey has a beginning, intermediate steps, and an end
- Each stage of the journey is broken down into steps—the activities you need to carry out

For example, let's consider the 'Convert' lifecycle stage. We need to identify the sources of opportunities and where they originated from because different opportunities may require different approaches. We may need to customise the conversations that our sales team members have with customers. The goal at this stage is not just to generate sales but to also generate quality sales that result in satisfied customers who progress to the next stage.

The stage after conversion may be 'Onboarding', the sources of which will be the customers who have completed the 'Convert' stage.

The customer journey is not always linear. Customers who have not converted and opportunities that have been marked as 'closed/lost' should not be overlooked. We may need to redirect these customers to a different stage of the customer lifecycle, or even a different product for down-selling or cross-selling. They could also become the audience for other marketing initiatives to keep them engaged until they are ready to make a purchase.

To document your CRM process, you need to know:

- Your customers are sourced from those who have achieved the milestones of preceding stages. Who are they?
- What is the milestone at the end of the stage? And where do customers go from there?
- Every customer needs to be progressing. What actions do they need to take to do so? What if they stall?
- What team or resources are available for each stage?
- What activities do those team members need to execute to keep customers progressing?
- What are the metrics you need to measure the performance of the team and the process?

Define the sources and resources, the actions and activities, and the milestones and metrics for every stage of the customer lifecycle.

Sources

The sources are the starting points for customers, showing where they came from before reaching their current stage. These could be channels such as cold outreach, events, lead magnets, webinars, social media, MQLs, or SQLs. Understanding the sources helps in customising approaches and monitoring conversion rates.

	Customers (External)	Team (Internal)
Start	Sources	Resources
Steps	Actions	Activities
End	Milestones	Metrics

Resources

Resources are our assets that guide customers at each stage, including team members, physical or digital sites, shops, or lead generation tools.

Actions

Actions represent the tasks customers need to complete as they progress through their journey. These tasks may include attending meetings, opening emails, signing contracts, visiting websites, registering, or downloading materials.

Activities

Activities are the internal tasks that a team must execute to keep customers engaged. This includes sending emails, scheduling meetings, inviting customers to events, and providing necessary contracts and other interactions.

Milestones

Milestones are important achievements that customers reach, marking the successful completion of stages. They represent the end of a stage in the customer journey and often become the starting point for subsequent stages.

Metrics

Metrics are internal performance indicators used to evaluate the effectiveness of each stage in the journey. These metrics include the number of sales, signups, and completed actions, providing measurable data to assess progress and success. From an internal perspective, we need to consider our resources, activities, and metrics. We'll discuss velocity later, as ensuring that every customer is constantly progressing is crucial. Additionally, not every customer will complete every stage. We must consider scenarios like leap, step, stall, and fall, and cater to each accordingly.

Every stage should be owned by one team. When different activities are owned by multiple teams within a process, accountability is lost. In addition, every customer within a stage should be assigned a team member.

Even if you don't implement all your pathways in your first phase build, it's important to identify where you will create pathways, as this helps the tech team understand how to configure and structure data to ensure you have the ability to move to the next phase without unnecessary re-work, while you continue to evolve and scale.

In any process pathway that you design, it's essential to define what the next action is AND an acceptable time period to complete the process.

This ensures you provide a consistent customer experience and leave nothing on the table.

The Leap, Step, Stall, Fall Model

As we design our CRM process, we outline the steps that most of our target customers will take to successfully reach their milestones at the end of each stage. However, thinking that all customers will reach the end is unrealistic. We need to consider different customer behaviours and outcomes and optimise our process for all these groups of customers. This is where the leap, step, stall, and fall model comes into play.

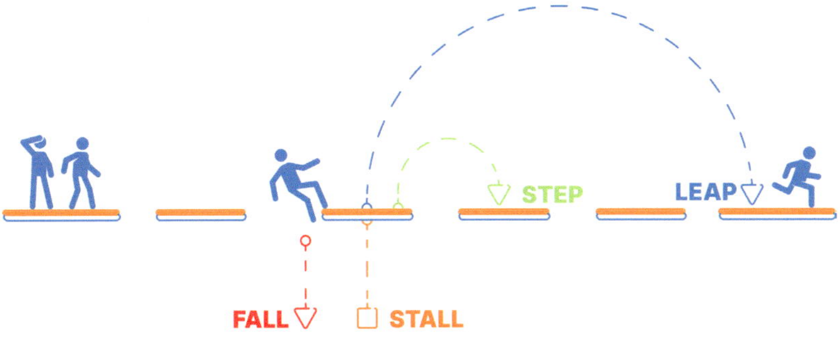

Consider all customer outcomes when mapping a journey

Leap:

Customers who prefer to skip steps and go straight to the end should be provided with the flexibility to expedite their journey. For example, in a conversion stage where customers are certain about making a purchase, offer a direct purchase option. This way, they won't have to go through the entire sales process, including engaging with salespeople and other steps. They can proceed directly to payment and purchase.

Step:

This represents the processes we design for the majority of our customers. We design a path with clear, actionable steps tailored to guide these customers through each stage. We ensure that each step adds value and leads them towards the milestone effectively. These steps are the focus of 99% of our CRM process mapping and strategy design. They are the default processes that efficiently guide our customers through their journey. These processes are the ones we need to continuously measure and optimise.

Stall:

Customers may encounter difficulties or experience delays in their progress along the journey. This can occur for various reasons, often when the customer fails to take the expected action. The simplest way to identify this is by calculating a velocity number or time-in-stage metric. For instance, if the average sales process takes 30 days, customers taking longer may be considered stalled and may require special attention. If a customer is not going to close, we need to move them out of this stage and place them into another pathway or nurturing journey for re-engagement.

Fall:

Not all customers will complete each stage of the process. This could be because they explicitly express disinterest in moving forward or because they take too long to make a decision and need to be guided to the next step. For instance, if a customer decides not to make a purchase, their status will be marked as a closed/lost opportunity. It's crucial to document the reason for this. If timing is the issue, you may opt to place them in a nurturing sequence to reconnect with them when they are ready to buy. In extreme cases, customers may clearly indicate that they no longer wish to engage with your business. In such instances, you should opt them out and refrain from targeting them in future marketing efforts—even if it means excluding them from lookalike audiences. This approach can enhance the results of future social media marketing activities.

Defining leap, step, stall, and fall are key metrics that matter and will be used to validate your journey mapping. When a customer stalls or falls, you need to consider what action needs to be taken to keep the customer moving toward the end goal.

The Product Journey Template

Our product journey template allows you to track and manage how customers move through the various lifecycle stages for each product type. It's intended to be simple, easily understood, non-technical, and quick to produce. It helps clarify which department is responsible for each stage, streamlining processes and enhancing customer interactions.

Throughout your product journey, you need to define steps that customers undertake on their journey when:

- They are getting to know you, as an audience in the 'Attract' stage
- You are getting to know them, while engaging with them as a prospect
- They like you, when marketing qualified as a lead while engaging with them
- They need you, when they become sales qualified and are an opportunity to convert
- They want you, and become a customer when they purchase the product, which you then fulfil
- They re-engage and buy more because you have retained them as a customer
- They love you, and start promoting you
- They lapse and lose interest, so you need to re-activate them
- They leave you—so you need to retire them from your marketing and systems gracefully

The product journey map isn't just about pushing customers through the sales funnel. It's about building relationships and delivering on promises. Whether it's a purchase, signing up for a service, or any other objective, you must provide value at every touchpoint.

When defining your product journey, refer to the key lifecycle stages and the information you need to store at each stage to maintain a single unified view of your customer.

For readability, we have provided three templates covering the three main phases of a product journey.

You may not need to replicate every single detail, action, and transaction in your platform. Key summaries such as 'has attended event' or invoice number and total invoice amount may be all you need to manage your customer relationships better.

The product matrix, hero journey, and product journey provide insight into how your products solve customer problems and allow you to see the big picture of how a customer might interact with your products.

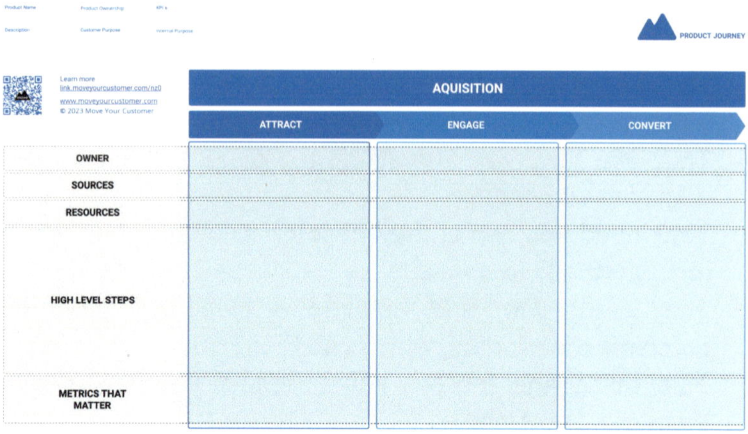

Figure 4: Product Journey—Acquisition Template

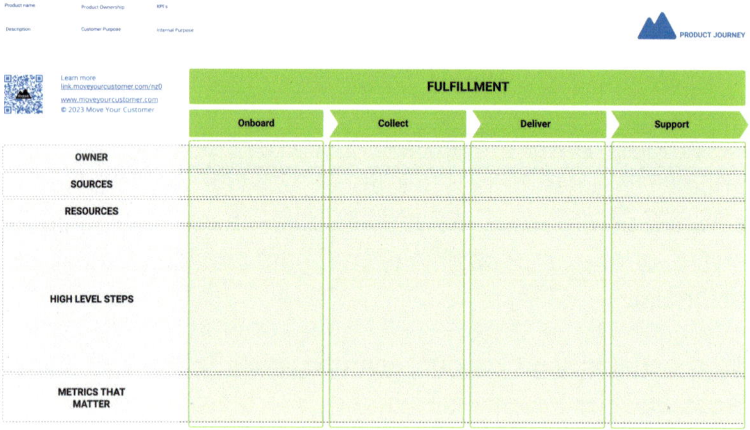

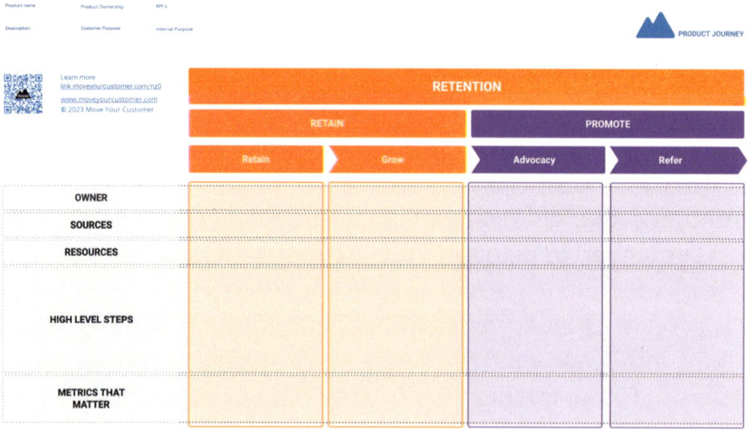

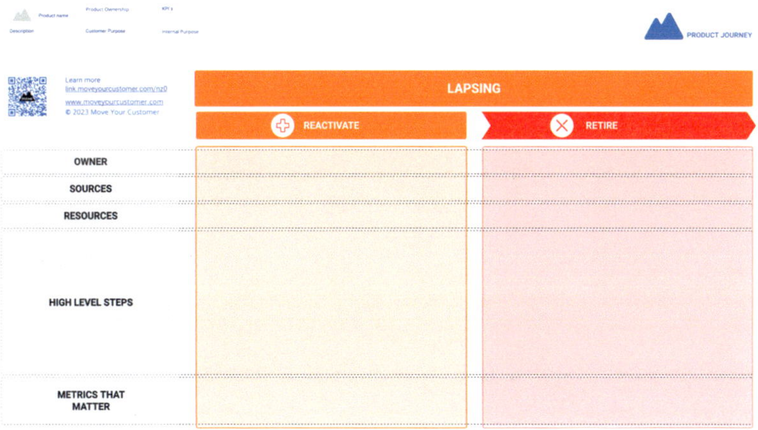

Who is your product for? This may relate to your qualifying questions

- Define what success is for your business with respect to this product
- Define what success looks like for your customer
- Define what leap, step, stall, and fall look like within that stage of the journey

This will help break down silos between teams by providing a shared understanding of the customer's journey.

The MOVE Canvas

The MOVE canvas helps you define the steps your customer must undertake (and the activities your team must perform) for the customer to keep progressing through to the end of a specific stage of their product journey.

Each MOVE canvas you create must connect to the next stage of the product journey. The customer destination of one canvas is the source of another. This cohesive integration will ensure that every customer interaction is aligned with your overarching strategy, keeping them engaged and delighted.

The MOVE canvas is not a standalone document; it is a breakdown of a stage of the product journey that delivers the detail of how to define the steps for each stage of the journey.

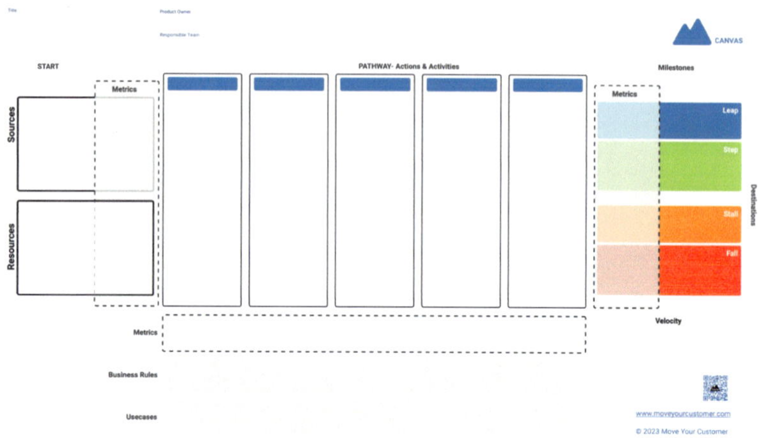

The MOVE Canvas Template

When drafting your process steps within the MOVE canvas, write them from the perspective of the customers' buying journey or from an internal process perspective. You need to choose which is the most appropriate for you and then make sure your steps are clear and consistent. For example: 'Looking to Purchase' (the customer perspective) or 'Qualifying' (the internal perspective)—but don't mix and match them.

Try and avoid the use of milestones when naming your steps. Rather, step names should be based on the activities or actions that are currently in progress. For example, use 'qualifying' rather than 'qualified'.

Each MOVE canvas you create must connect to the next stage of the product journey. The customer destinations of one canvas are the source of another. This cohesive integration will ensure that every customer interaction aligns with your overarching strategy, keeping them engaged and delighted.

But more than this, the MOVE canvas:

- Provides the context of how your processes and pathways fit in the overall customer journey by identifying where your customers come from and what they need to achieve. We call these your sources and milestones.
- Establishes who is accountable for the pathway outcomes by identifying ownership and who the process owners are.

Ownership and allocating accountability are the number one reasons CRM implementation fails. The next chapter, O is for Ownership, covers this in detail.

- Captures the metrics to give visibility over how your processes are performing. We go into more detail in the V is for Visibility chapter later in the book.

Your MOVE canvas serves as both a comprehensive requirements document and a streamlined standard operating procedure. Importantly, it should contain the necessary details to concisely communicate to a technical CRM administrator the specific implementation required.

Remember, don't just replicate existing processes. This is your chance to improve the customer experience, not replicate how you do things now. Don't be defined by how things are done, create new, better ways of doing things, and agree on how you want to manage and track every step.

Use Cases

Each canvas is made up of a number of steps you need to guide your customer through. In fact, you have now captured your business processes in a format that can be implemented on your CRM platform.

Each step exists for a reason. We often call these reasons a 'use case'. It describes a 'usage scenario' or how something should be used. A use case sets out why we are doing something, who is doing it, and what they are doing. Each use case refers to a scenario or situation that describes how a user interacts with the CRM platform to achieve a particular objective. They are very simple and can be laid out by completing a simple sentence that reads:

> *As an X, I want to do Y so that I can get a Z result.*

Use cases are important because they identify who is doing what within the CRM platform and for what purpose.

Use cases help identify:

- Specific interactions between technical and functional processes
- Improvements in the usefulness of a system
- Ways to improve and manage expectations
- How to determine the best possible outcome scenario and steer clear of implementation risks

A comprehensive list of use cases is the foundation for documenting your CRM platform requirements. They explain the desired functionality within the context of your specific business.

They help provide more context to the development team on each step within the pathway and can also be the basis of your user acceptance testing (UAT). This will help validate and determine if your system has been configured correctly, given your business requirements.

Use cases are easy to collect. The team member who owns the pathway (the process) needs to capture them.

Let's run through an example:

Step	**Book a Sales Meeting**
As a...	Sales representative
I want to...	Book a sales call
So that...	I can present an offer
What information do I need?	The company name and details, the decision maker's contact details, and how they engaged with our company
What do I do?	Send an introductory email with a meeting request. If not accepted, follow up with a call. After three contact attempts, close the opportunity and set the closed/lost reason to 'uncontactable send reactivation emails'. If the meeting request is accepted, change the opportunity stage to 'sales meeting scheduled'.

Unfortunately, in our experience, this is often where momentum is lost.

The business gets excited about defining their high-level product journey and having a clear vision of what they want, however, they do not allocate the time to complete the MOVE canvas.

'The devil is in the detail; you need to keep moving and take the time to document the steps within each stage of the product journey.

This is where you really need to challenge your current ways of working, and redefine how you want things to work, to provide the best possible customer experience and move away from manual and disjointed internal processes.

This document is the blueprint of your build and provides the technical team or partner with the exact requirements of how to configure your CRM platform.

O IS FOR OWNERSHIP

OWNERSHIP

Ownership is arguably the most important aspect in determining the success of your CRM investment.

Ownership goes beyond mere responsibility; it requires deep involvement and control over tasks and processes. To cultivate this sense of ownership within your team, it's essential to define clear roles and responsibilities for your CRM platform and processes.

"Responsibility equals accountability equals ownership. And a sense of ownership is the most powerful weapon a team or organisation can have." – Pat Summitt

Doing so will empower team members and lead to better collaboration, enhanced efficiency, and a commitment to quality. Furthermore, it will facilitate faster problem-solving and empower change management efforts, which in turn will drive continuous improvement and a successful implementation.

Here's why ownership matters:

- Defined ownership encourages collaboration among teams, fostering a transparent approach to tasks and processes
- With ownership, tasks have designated leaders, reducing confusion and potential conflict, leading to greater efficiency
- Ownership creates a commitment to excellence, with individuals striving for the success of their processes
- Clear ownership leads to faster problem-solving when issues arise, saving time and resources

- Owners are best placed to empower change management efforts, driving successful improvements and changes
- Knowing who owns what ensures resources are streamlined and dedicated where they're most needed and used effectively

Shared responsibility is no responsibility

Ownership empowers individuals and departments, signifying the trust and authority needed to make changes and improvements. This empowerment drives the business towards its goals and strengthens the bond between employees and their responsibilities.

Understanding Accountability

Being accountable is linked to taking ownership. The individual who is accountable is the one who is responsible for the end result.

They must report on key performance indicators (KPI), and if they fail to meet them, even if they were delegated to someone else, they are responsible for identifying and resolving any issues.

"You can delegate responsibility, but you cannot delegate accountability." – Byron Dorgan

The RACI Matrix

The RACI matrix is an invaluable project management tool used to define and communicate roles and responsibilities within a project or process. It stands for Responsible, Accountable, Consulted, and Informed.

Responsible (R):

This role belongs to the person or people responsible for executing a specific task or activity. They perform the work.

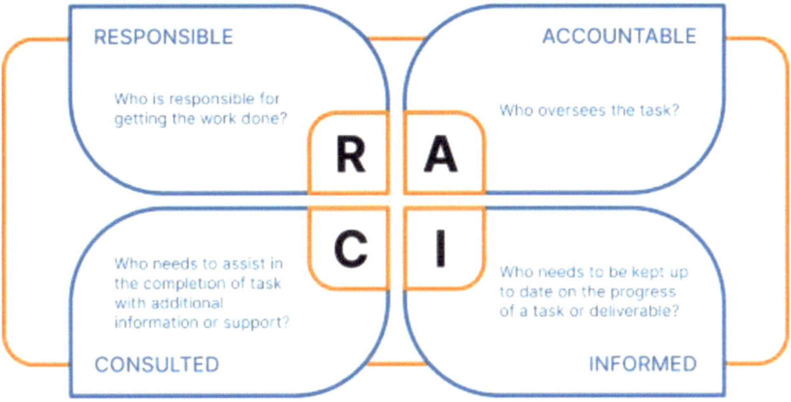

The RACI Matrix

Accountable (A):

The role is ultimately answerable for the final outcome and results. They are the decision-makers with the authority to approve or sign off on the work performed by the 'Responsible' individual(s).

Consulted (C):

Individuals or stakeholders in this role provide input, guidance, or expertise. They are subject matter experts or key stakeholders who offer valuable insights.

Informed (I):

The people or groups in this role need to be kept informed about progress and results but are not directly involved in execution. Regular updates ensure transparency and awareness of any developments.

The RACI matrix is a powerful tool that ensures everyone understands their role and responsibilities. It prevents confusion and clarifies decision-making authority while enhancing communication and collaboration within the team.

Levels of Ownership

Consider ownership at four different levels:

- The product or product journey
- The pathway or stage
- The customer
- The platform

Product Ownership

The product owner takes a key role as they are responsible for overseeing the development and management of a product or service. The product owner serves as the liaison between the business, customers, and development teams, ensuring that the product aligns with customer needs and business goals.

In medium-sized businesses, the role of product ownership is often overlooked, and there is often no one person clearly responsible for a product's performance.

Every product has to have someone who is monitoring how that product is performing overall in the business. This includes the marketing and sales numbers related to that product.

Let's explore the significance of product ownership and its role in defining successful product paths within your CRM platform.

The Role of the Product Owner

Every product needs a product owner who takes ownership of defining the product pathway and aligning expected outcomes with the product's purpose.

When introducing a new product, the product owner must consider how it will be tracked and implemented into your CRM platform.

Key considerations for the product owner include:

- The Product's Fit within your Hero Journey: Determine where every product fits within the hero journey and map where customers are coming from and going to after they purchase your product

- Defining the Product Journey and Pathways: Clearly define the customer's journey through the product journey, including different stages and steps
- Reusing Existing Pathways: Assess whether existing pathways can be reused or if new pathways are needed for the new product
- Changes and Optimisations in your CRM: Identify any changes or optimisations required to accommodate the new product
- Monitor KPIs related to the product: This doesn't just mean customer satisfaction, but also sales, conversions, retention, and cross-selling to other products

The product owner is accountable and responsible for how the product works within the CRM platform. Their role ensures seamless integration of the product journey with the overall customer journey.

Product KPIs and Processes

The product owner is responsible for defining the Key Performance Indicators (KPIs) for the team and processes associated with each product journey. It is critical to understand what it takes for each team to guide a customer through each stage of the product journey.

Without clear product ownership and defined processes, your products may become siloed. This hinders your ability to maximise the value of your customer relationships and leads to disconnected systems and inefficiencies, resulting in a fragmented and poor customer experience.

Process Ownership

CRM Process is defining a customer's steps through a particular stage of a product journey. We discuss this in detail during the chapter 'M is Map'.

The MOVE canvas represents the steps between stages of a customer journey. It is your customer pathway.

A step on the pathway represents the activities that need to be carried out to keep your customer progressing down that pathway to the next stage. A pathway is owned by a person (a manager) or a team (the sales team).

Each owner has the responsibility and accountability to manage and optimise their business processes from start to finish. This includes everything from designing and implementing the steps in the process to continuously improving and monitoring their performance.

For example: each stage of the product journey, known as a pathway, may be owned by a different team. The marketing team may be responsible for attracting leads and qualifying them for sales. Marketing owns the 'attract' stage and must clearly define the steps a customer or internal team needs to take in order to progress to the next stage.

To successfully own a pathway means:

- Understanding the Process: You have a detailed understanding and control of the process, knowing its goals, inputs, outputs, and key performance indicators (KPIs).
- Ensuring Efficiency and Effectiveness: You focus on making the process as efficient and effective as possible, so it aligns with the organisation's overall goals.
- Identifying Improvement Opportunities: You are always on the lookout for ways to make things better, by spotting bottlenecks, inefficiencies, and areas that need a boost.
- Collaborating with Others: You work closely with the people involved, ensuring everyone knows what they're responsible for. But you also need to collaborate with the teams responsible for other stages in the customer's journey.

- Implementing Changes: When there are better ways of doing things, you ensure those changes happen and monitor how they affect the process.
- Monitoring Performance: You keep an eye on how the process is doing, using KPIs to measure what's going well and what might need some attention.

By giving clear ownership of specific business processes, organisations can make people more accountable, make decisions faster, and build a culture of continuous improvement. And that leads to increased efficiency and effectiveness in the ways that people work together.

Customer Ownership

Customer ownership plays a pivotal role in ensuring the ultimate success of your customer and CRM strategy.

Having a customer champion within your business ensures the focus stays on the customer and not on short-term gains or operational convenience. The easier option is not always the best for the customer.

How does customer ownership translate into concrete action? Imagine a scenario in which every department, from sales to marketing, and customer support to product development, views themselves as custodians of the customer's journey. In such a scenario:

- Marketing doesn't just create campaigns; they craft experiences that resonate deeply.
- Salespeople don't just close deals; they establish long-term relationships.
- Customer support teams don't just solve problems; they become partners in success.
- Product development doesn't just create products; they create perfect solutions
- Each department becomes a custodian of the customer's journey, fostering genuine value.

- Your CRM platform stands as the conduit through which this ownership flows.

The Head of Customer

A senior individual, such as the Head of Customer or Head of Marketing, needs to own the ultimate success of the business's customer and CRM platform strategy. They serve as the voice of the customer and the champion of the customer-centric approach within the organisation. This individual is responsible for aligning the CRM strategy with business goals and ensuring the platform optimises customer interactions.

Individuals/Team Members/Users

Within each department team, individuals are given ownership of every customer or step in the process. In a system like Salesforce, every record has an owner who is responsible for keeping the record's progress through its stages, steps, or processes. Having a clear sense of ownership ensures that each customer's journey is well-managed and progresses smoothly through the stages of the product journey.

Platform Ownership

A CRM platform often becomes the infrastructure that powers your customer-centric business processes. While IT is responsible for the technical elements of CRM for instance, the platform's ownership should lie within your business functions. The senior person responsible for your CRM strategy should own and be accountable for integrating the system into your operations.

Platform Owner

This is a business-facing role, responsible for defining and delivering the CRM roadmap so that it is aligned with your business objectives. This individual reports to the Head of Customer, engages with the business, defines product features, prioritises the product backlog, and collaborates with the CRM administrator (the technical owner) to ensure the platform's success.

Department SMEs (Subject Matter Experts)

Within each department, identify a subject matter expert (SME) as the department representative involved in all CRM platform development and optimisation aspects. Working collaboratively with the CRM platform owner, the SME ensures their team's processes align with the customer, product journeys, and pathways.

V IS FOR VISIBILITY

VISIBILITY

Visibility is the third principle of MOVE. It emphasises the importance of having clear, measurable objectives—and the means to track them.

So now that you have defined your customer journeys through your products and identified who is accountable for every step of your processes (and documented these), it is time to focus on how you manage these business processes effectively.

This statement forms the cornerstone of modern management practice. Having quantifiable goals and metrics makes it easier to measure progress.

To understand whether your processes yield the desired outcomes, you must define and track what success looks like. It needs to be quantified. And visible.

To ensure successful reporting and tracking, it is essential to take the time to define what needs to be measured and to clearly communicate this to your technical team.

Delaying reporting to subsequent phases can lead to rework for the development team, additional costs for the business, and a frustrated senior management team.

The What, Who, and How of Metrics

To ensure visibility in your business, three essential elements must be considered.

Firstly, it's important to identify WHAT needs to be measured, including KPIs, leading and lagging measures, and the impact of inputs.

Secondly, it's crucial to determine WHO needs to know this information. We have a simple hierarchical model to explain this. We call this our EXTREME metrics model.

Finally, you need to know HOW to measure this data, which can be achieved through reports and dashboards.

What Needs to Be Measured

Goals: Goals are critical for managing your business effectively. They can be ongoing performance-based goals or overarching strategic goals. The SMART rule is useful for defining any goal:

- Specific
- Measurable
- Achievable
- Relevant
- Time-bound

KPIs: KPIs are quantifiable measures of performance over time for a specific objective. They provide targets for teams, milestones to gauge progress, and insights to help decision-making across your organisation. KPIs should align with the stages of your customer journey and the current stage of their lifecycle.

"You can't manage what you can't measure."
– Peter Drucker

There is a lot of literature on the theory related to this subject, so we are only going to touch on the fundamentals of defining KPIs.

We are using the term KPIs generically. In your organisation, you may have different terms.

Leading and Lagging Measures

KPIs are often a combination of leading and lagging measures.

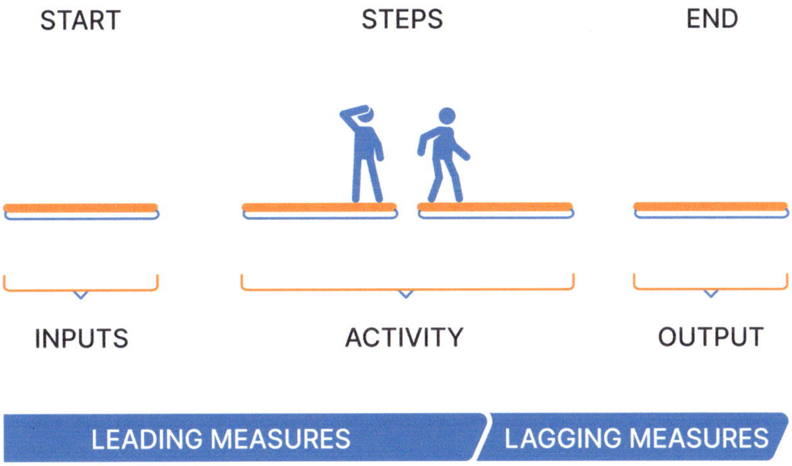

Leading measures help predict lagging measures

Lagging Measures

Lagging measures are the outcomes or results of your business activities. They reflect past performance. Examples of lagging measures include total revenue, net profit, customer churn rate, market share, and ROI. They provide a snapshot of your efforts and interactions and help create a vision of where you want your organisation to be in the future.

Lagging measures are often goal numbers. They tell what you achieved in a period. For example, the number of sales in the quarter or the conversion rate for that quarter.

And this is why leading measures are so important. They are predictors of future results.

Leading Measures

Leading measures are predictive numbers that help you anticipate future lagging numbers. They lead you to your results by showing you your progress.

Divide your leading measures into:

- **Inputs** are what you were given at the start of the process, often beyond your control. For example: 'The sales team is expecting 500 opportunities to be created each month'. Or 'Marketing will deliver 1,000 new leads'.
- **Activities** are the things you do as part of your processes to convert inputs into outputs. Leading measures offer direct control over these activities. For example, tracking the number of daily calls and meetings by each team member.
- **Outputs** are a combination of the inputs you received, the activities you have undertaken, and the results these two activities have yielded.

Leading and Lagging Measures Case Study

Last year, the marketing team generated 12,000 qualified opportunities for the five sales team members.

The process to convert customers (the customer pathway) involves making outbound calls and asking a series of 'discovery' questions.

On average, every client is called twice. If a client shows interest, a proposal is issued for the client to accept. In the past year, they were able to generate:

- $12,000,000 in revenue from 12,000 sales. This averages out to 100 sales with an average order value of $10,000. This year, they want to achieve the same.

Their conversion rate is 10%. They win 10% of all qualified opportunities created by marketing. Conversion rate is the number of won sales divided by the number of opportunities created. It tells us how the sales team is performing.

Halfway through the current year, they look at their sales numbers. Instead of reaching 600 sales, they have only made 300. They are half of what they expected.

For the sales team to reach their target of 1,200 sales for the year, they must now make 900 sales in the second half of the year to catch up. This means that marketing will have

to create more opportunities, and the sales team will need to expand their size to make the additional calls required to achieve the target.

Leading measures provide early warning indicators and allow us to take action soon. Let's look at a couple of scenarios:

- If the conversion rate is still 10%, then the sales team is performing as expected and it is likely that the marketing team under delivered the number of leads to the sales team. The number of opportunities created should be tracked daily as a leading source or input metric.

If the conversion rate fell to 5%, then it's more likely there was a performance problem in the sales team. We'd look at:

1. The sales team members. If there had been churn in the team, maybe we need to improve the training.

2. If the number of calls being made daily had also dropped by half, we would look to see if there was a breakdown in our sales process.

3. If the number of calls being made was unchanged and there had been no change in the sales team, it's possible that the quality of the opportunities were not of a high quality.

Types of Metrics on Dashboards

Numbers rarely make sense in isolation, so dashboards often present multiple metrics to provide context and enable effective analysis. There are different types of metrics to consider:

- Absolute Numbers: These are straightforward counts or totals, providing concrete measures of specific aspects of your business or performance.
- Relative Numbers: These offer ratios, percentages, or comparisons to provide a more nuanced understanding of performance. They enable context by comparing one metric to another or against a benchmark.
- Comparative Numbers: These show comparisons to the same time in a different period or between different territories, helping you identify what is considered as normal.
- Target Numbers: These represent specific goals or objectives set for a particular metric, providing a clear target to strive for and enabling progress tracking.
- The Period: This refers to the point in time and the period over which you are measuring, such as monthly, quarterly, or for the last financial year.
- Cumulative Numbers: While you might report performance within a specific period (e.g., monthly), cumulative numbers offer an overview of performance over time.

A well-designed dashboard balances absolute and relative numbers, providing stakeholders with a comprehensive view of performance. When you incorporate both measures, dashboards become powerful tools for monitoring progress, making data-driven decisions, and fostering a culture of continuous improvement.

By maintaining visibility and clarity of objectives through well-defined KPIs and metrics, you can effectively manage your business, track progress, and ensure that your customer strategies lead to successful outcomes.

Who is Responsible
The EXTREME Metrics Dashboard Model

Let's dive into the importance of visibility and accountability, and who needs to see what?

Our EXTREME metrics dashboard model is a cascading model of metrics whenever you need to produce KPIs and dashboards for your CRM processes.

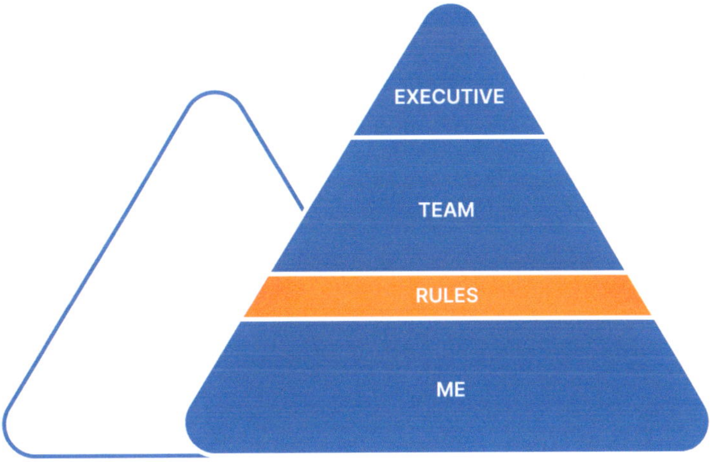

Extreme Metrics

As business leaders and decision-makers, you know that success is driven by quantifiable goals and metrics. It's challenging to gauge progress and make data-driven decisions without looking into your processes' performance. That's why anything you implement into your CRM platform MUST have an accompanying dashboard with relevant reports of your leading and lagging measures.

O

Every dashboard must be assigned an owner. They are accountable for reporting and acting on the numbers in the dashboard.

Just because you can measure everything does not mean everyone needs to know. You should only share the metrics that matter with the people who are in a position to influence the outcomes. If you present a dashboard with thousands of numbers, it becomes meaningless. You only have to show the metrics that matter.

The EXTREME hierarchical metrics model is a straightforward and powerful framework that ensures everyone in your organisation stays aligned with company KPIs and goals from top to bottom.

EXTREME is a four-level metrics model

- **EX**: Executive level
- **T**: Team level
- **R**: Rules and adherence to business processes
- **ME**: Individual performance

The EXECUTIVE Level Dashboards

At the executive level, you need to have a dashboard displaying the highest-level KPIs. These are the key metrics that give a snapshot of how the company is progressing toward its goals.

Typically, these will be the key lagging measures for every team, process, or product.

For example:

- Leads generated by marketing
- Sales revenue and sales conversion rate
- Customer satisfaction

At an executive level, the board or owners want to see the actual results, at a glance, in as near to real-time as possible. This dashboard becomes the go-to reference for executive meetings, giving you a real-time overview of company performance.

If numbers are above or below target, you can drill down to a team level to see how the team delivered on their leading measures—those activities (like sales calls) need to be actioned daily to achieve their goals.

The TEAM Level Dashboards

Just like a sports team, your team needs to know the score. So, you need to have a scoreboard that tracks their wins. These goal numbers are usually key lagging metrics the whole team is striving to achieve in the period.

But your scoreboard also needs to show how they are performing. How efficient and effective are they? Are the results representative of their actual performance, or are there external factors driving poor performance?

Team dashboards offer a comprehensive view of how your team has performed and the reasons behind that performance.

Lagging measures for team dashboards can include:

- Target Achievement: This refers to the specific goals or benchmarks your team needs to hit to be considered successful. It's crucial to define these targets clearly, ensuring they align with your broader business objectives.
- Current Score vs. Target: This shows where your team currently stands in relation to the set goals. It's a direct measure of progress and success, helping you understand if you are on track or need to adjust your strategies.
- Team Performance: Performance measurement is about measuring effectiveness and efficiency. It's not just about whether targets are being met but also how they are being achieved. Performance measures are typically one metric divided by another. For example, conversion rate, calls per day, and average sale value. These measures help identify areas for improvement or reinforcement.

Leading measures for team dashboards can include:

Sources:

- Input Sufficiency: Evaluate if your team has received the necessary inputs (like leads, information, tools) to reach their targets.
- Input Quality: Assess whether the quality of these inputs is high enough to facilitate reaching your targets.

Resources:

- Resource Requirements: Identify the resources (human, technological, financial) needed for your team to meet its objectives. Think of it as determining the ideal team composition and support.
- Resource Availability and Performance: Examine the resources currently available to your team and evaluate if they are performing optimally. Are these resources meeting expectations, and if not, why?

Activities:

- Operational Execution: Are team members actively engaged in the necessary tasks? This includes making calls, responding to cases, raising quotes, and other CRM activities.
- Activity Metrics: These metrics help you track whether your team is effectively carrying out the steps required in the customer pathway.

The Business RULES Dashboard

Business rule dashboards give you trust in your data and processes.

Trust in your data is paramount; it forms the foundation on which you make crucial decisions. So, it's important to know you can trust the data on which your metrics are based.

To do this, you need to define your business rules. And for each rule, create a report or metric that monitors how this rule is being followed.

Data can go wrong in two primary ways:

- Incorrect Data Entry: This occurs when fields are left incomplete or incorrect values are entered manually. Thankfully, such issues can be identified and corrected through validation rules and standardised pick lists (rather than free text) during data entry.

- Process Non-Compliance: Tracking and enforcing compliance becomes challenging when users deviate from established processes. However, monitoring defined business rules can help address this challenge effectively.

For example, every opportunity in your CRM should have a close date. Therefore, you need to show the number of opportunities where the close date for open opportunities is in the past. Beyond this, each sales team member needs to see their own open opportunities where the close date has already passed and has not been updated.

It's easier than you think to ensure data accuracy, especially when you use the MOVE methodology. After creating a path process map, you'll know which specific data points are crucial for managing activities and progress—for each step of the process. Defining the business rules around each data point and turning each one into a report will give you the visibility you need to ensure your processes are running as designed.

Remember, adhering to well-defined business rules ensures the accuracy and reliability of your data, leading to better decision-making and improved overall performance.

The 'ME' Dashboard

The 'ME' level in the EXTREME model focuses on individual performance, using individual dashboards. In today's fast-paced business environment, effectively managing tasks and juggling multiple responsibilities is crucial. That's where personalised dashboards come in, offering individual team members a powerful tool with which to boost productivity and track performance. This can include things like:

Daily Tasks: A clear and concise overview of daily tasks allows team members to prioritise their work, plan their day, and efficiently stay on top of progress. Visualising daily responsibilities ensures nothing falls through the cracks.

Top Deals: Having a 'Top Deals' section is important for sales and business development teams. It helps to draw attention to the most promising opportunities, keeping team members focused on important goals and motivating them to contribute to the success of the business.

Leaderboards: A friendly leaderboard that compares team members and fosters a positive, high-performance culture. Recognising achievements and offering visibility into everyone's performance promotes healthy competition and collaboration within the team.

Data Clean-Up: Accurate data is crucial, and a data clean-up section helps manage information quality. Highlight data discrepancies to the owners of those records so they can be rectified.

Progress Toward Goals: Track progress toward individual goals using charts and graphs.

Efficiency Measures: Analysing the task completion speed and the success rate helps optimise workflows and resource allocation.

These personalised dashboards empower team members to understand their strengths, identify areas for improvement, and align their efforts with broader goals. This fosters a culture of accountability, collaboration, and growth.

E IS FOR EVOLUTION

E EVOLUTION

When implementing a CRM platform, the goal is to have a single view of the customer across their entire lifecycle and all products. However, it's unrealistic to expect to implement a new CRM with all its features, processes, products, teams, and historical customer data across all sources in a single project. This level of digital transformation is highly unlikely to be successful.

The ideal approach is to map out the customer lifecycle using the high-level product journey template. You can then break this down into smaller projects and prioritise them. This provides a roadmap for your transformation journey with CRM, enabling you to deliver business value quickly by focusing on the highest priority stages first. Performance improvements today finance future improvements tomorrow, enabling you to deliver the next highest priority.

During implementation, you'll find that the lifecycle nature of CRM naturally leads you to focus on the stage immediately before or after the one you've just transformed. Solving one problem often reveals the next underlying problem. For example, if you need to improve your sales conversion rate as the highest priority, you may improve the sales team's conversion rate by implementing a better sales process, only to find that it highlights poor quality leads being converted into opportunities. The next phase may then focus on better qualifying leads, and this continually expands the scope of your implementation to cover all aspects of the customer lifecycle.

Failing to plan properly often means not taking into account the entire customer lifecycle, which can result in having to go back and redo the initial setup. This oversight can occur when certain nuances in the product, structure, opportunities, marketing, and customer service are not considered. Many CRM platforms are initially set up to tackle a specific challenge that the business may be dealing with at a particular point in time (e.g., sales) and usually only focus on one part of the customer lifecycle. If the customer lifecycle is not properly mapped out, this can lead to much bigger problems down the line. For example:

- Teams not being in sync with changes in the company
- Not planning for future or earlier needs in the journey

A real-life example of this might be the marketing team launching a new financial reward incentive without considering the entire client lifecycle, causing problems for the accounts team during billing. Therefore, the most crucial step when starting a new CRM implementation is to map out your customer and product journeys and then prioritise where to begin. Your customer journey should serve as your implementation roadmap over time. It's vital to treat CRM implementation as an ongoing process that is evolving continually. Implement in small, manageable chunks, iterating and expanding constantly, rather than aiming for a single, comprehensive launch.

Small and medium enterprises (SMEs) often operate differently from large enterprises, as they are typically owner driven. While they may lack the mature processes and structures of larger counterparts, this can be an advantage, allowing them to move swiftly and adapt quickly. However, with this agility comes the need to change at a pace that matches their capabilities and resources.

When considering your CRM implementation strategy, there are two really important principles:

1. CRM implementation is a constant evolution
2. Evolve at a pace that matches your capability, maturity, and resources.

Evolution, Not Revolution:

CRM implementation is a continuous process—not a big bang project.

- A Journey is Made of Many Steps. Most companies initially implement CRM to solve a specific problem. It could be to improve sales, customer engagement, or service delivery. Regardless of where you start, always map your Product Journey to understand the entire customer lifecycle, your qualification criteria, the team, the processes and the interactions with customers. Then focus on your pain point and implement solutions in the context of the entire lifecycle. Then move on to your next pain point, but always in the context of the Product Journey.
- Be Agile: Business priorities change. Often, you must implement a tactical fix to solve an urgent problem. But it's essential to keep referring to and updating your product journey map and your product journey strategic outcome.
- Prioritise for Maximum Impact: Make strategic decisions on what to implement next based on your capability, resources, and budget. Focus on what matters most and align tasks with your strategic goals.
- Be Business-Led: Ensure decisions are rooted in the broader business context and strategy. Maintain a sense of ownership throughout the implementation process. Make sure you deliver results early and rapidly.

Match your pace with your capability.

Your CRM implementation must evolve at a pace that matches your capability, maturity, and resources.

Small and medium-sized enterprises operate differently from large enterprises. Unlike organisations with boards, shareholders, and directors to answer to, you are typically owner-driven. You may lack your larger counterparts' mature processes and structures, but this can give you a unique advantage.

You can move swiftly, adapt with ease, and embrace the occasional messiness that comes with your agile nature. It's a world where perfection takes a backseat to progress and where opportunities are seized without hesitation.

However, the pace at which you evolve must match your capability and resources (time, money, and people) to manage that change.

Maturity

Organisational maturity plays a significant role in determining how a technical solution should be delivered. For instance, there is no point in implementing a fully integrated marketing automation platform if your current and future marketing strategy only consists of sending out a monthly email and a weekly social media post. You need to at least have a basic process in place to understand how to implement marketing automations. Evolution is about implementing a tactical solution to solve an immediate problem today, knowing full well that you will revisit this in a year or two.

Resources

When planning your CRM implementation, evaluate the resources you have at your disposal. Simply put, what time, money, and people do you have to invest?

Time is one of the most critical resources. Implementing a CRM system isn't an overnight task; it requires a substantial time commitment from your team.

Consider the following aspects when allocating time:

Initial Setup: Time needed for the initial configuration of the CRM platform, including setting up data structures, workflows, and user permissions.

- Data Migration: Transferring existing customer data into the new CRM system, ensuring data accuracy and integrity.

- Training: Time for training your team to effectively use the CRM system, including both initial training and ongoing education as new features and updates are introduced.
- Ongoing Management: Regular maintenance tasks such as data cleaning, system updates, and performance monitoring.

Planning realistic timelines and milestones helps in managing expectations and ensuring that the project stays on track.

Money

Financial resources are always a factor. A CRM implementation involves many cost components, and budgeting appropriately ensures that you can sustain the project from start to finish. Consider these financial aspects:

Software Licences: Costs for purchasing or subscribing to the CRM platform. This can vary based on the number of users, the level of functionality required, the amount of data or processing, and whether the software is cloud-based or on-premises. Make sure to estimate what your license costs will be as adoption and usage grows.

- Implementation Costs: Fees for consultants or implementation partners who assist with the initial setup and customisation of the CRM system.
- Training Programmes: Costs associated with training your team, which might include hiring trainers, purchasing training materials, or subscribing to online training platforms.
- Ongoing Costs: Recurring expenses such as subscription renewals, support contracts, and any additional features or modules you might need as your CRM system evolves.

People

Human resources are equally important. The success of your CRM implementation largely depends on the people involved:

Project Team: A dedicated project team that includes members from various departments such as IT, sales, marketing, and customer service. This team will oversee the implementation process, ensuring that all aspects of the CRM system meet the needs of different business units.

- CRM Champions: Key individuals who are passionate about the CRM system and can act as advocates within the organisation. They play a critical role in driving user adoption and ensuring that the CRM system is used effectively.
- Technical Support: Skilled IT professionals who can manage the technical aspects of the CRM system, including customisation, integration with other systems, and troubleshooting.
- External Consultants: If you lack certain expertise in-house, external consultants can provide the necessary skills and knowledge to ensure a successful implementation.

It is crucial to ensure that your internal business users have the time and focus necessary to fully engage in the implementation process. Their support and buy-in are essential for the success of the project.

Capability

The more capable you are, the faster you can evolve. Invest in building up your in-house ability to manage your CRM system. By doing so, you are investing in a strategy and a platform that will transform your business. Make sure you have the skills to manage the solution you have, or you will not maximise the return on your time and financial investment.

Just as you would train your operators on specialised manufacturing machinery, ensure that you train your operators and have technical support available to configure and maintain your CRM platform. You need someone on the business side to own the processes and customer data, and someone on the technical side to configure and maintain the platform. You can also choose to contract out these technical resources, but you cannot contract out business ownership.

When you have selected a platform, commit to investing in the training first. This will lift your capability and give you the skills and language to better articulate your requirements. Too often, training follows implementation. If you know the capabilities of the software upfront, you can design your processes better.

Assign ownership of your CRM and processes and ensure that the individuals have the capability to operate, improve, and maintain them.

The Roles in CRM

It's important to understand the different roles required to operate, maintain, and improve your CRM as your business evolves. Let's break down these roles.

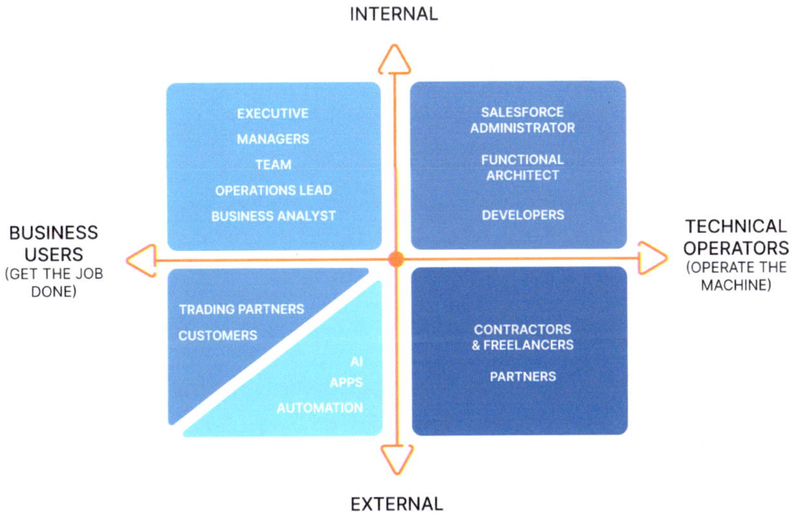

On one side, you have business users. They have business-focused roles that drive daily operations and use CRM from an operational perspective.

This group includes executives, managers, and team members. Their main goal is to align the CRM system with business objectives and provide feedback on its functionality.

On the flip side, there are technical operators. They have technology-focused roles to ensure the platform's technical soundness and alignment with business needs.

This segment is spearheaded by the CRM administrator, but for more extensive organisations, it may expand to include architects and developers.

Then, there are hybrid roles like business analysts. They bridge the gap, translating business needs into technical requirements and ensuring project alignment.

Sometimes, external expertise is necessary. Companies might seek external resources, such as contractors, CRM vendor partners, or trading partners, for specialised input or collaboration.

The balance between internal and external resources depends on each business's unique needs, size, objectives, and budget. The ultimate goal: a cohesive team driving business growth on the CRM platform.

But it's really important to note that, whilst you can contract out technical support, you can never contract out business ownership of the processes and data.

The CRM Administrator

A CRM administrator is a non-negotiable role for any business implementing CRM. CRM administrators build, configure, and automate technology solutions to meet business needs and solve problems.

The CRM administrator works alongside the CRM platform owner and the subject matter experts to define system requirements. The CRM administrator customises the platform accordingly. It is critical to have them involved in the project from the beginning and to document key developments as the solution is being designed and delivered.

Collaboration and alignment between the CRM platform owner, CRM administrator, and the implementation partner are crucial for a successful CRM implementation. External partners can bring best practices and expertise, but the internal team's understanding of the business is vital for a successful solution.

Working with Implementation Partners:

Companies often rely heavily on implementation partners to set up the platform for them, resulting in situations where they have all the necessary tools but lack the knowledge or capability to fully utilise the platform.

The ultimate objective when collaborating with a partner is to seamlessly transition into full operation once implementation is complete. This involves assuming complete control of the solution, effectively managing the system, and achieving the desired business outcomes.

To do this, you must:

- Build your own capability to manage the solution before the solution goes live. Identify who in the business will be the solution owner and will be responsible for delivering the outcomes you planned
- Prioritise learning and training to ensure a successful implementation. It's crucial for you and your team to prioritise learning and training from the outset
- Engage in training up front. Even before you begin to outline a solution, training allows you to familiarise yourselves with the platform's terminology and grasp its software functionalities and constraints.

- This will equip you to express your requirements more effectively and accurately during the scoping phase, enhancing your ability to define what you need from the platform in a practical and realistic manner—and also what you don't need!
- Define your own requirements. Taking a proactive approach to defining requirements is an important step for a successful implementation. Relying solely on partners can lead to miscommunication and dependence, so clearly define processes early on to ensure team understanding and articulation of workflows and needs. This lays the foundation for a smoother implementation, tailoring solutions to meet specific requirements.
- Take the lead. When working with a partner, have your team take the lead and allow the partner to provide guidance. This approach helps your team gain hands-on experience and become self-reliant. This maximises your team's involvement and confidence while leveraging the partner's expertise.

Finding a Partner

As most businesses lack the technical expertise to implement a CRM platform independently, most vendors will introduce you to implementation partners as part of their onboarding process.

When engaging with implementation partners, consider the following steps:

- Look for partners with a proven track record, positive client testimonials, and a strong understanding of your industry challenges.
- Request detailed proposals that outline their approach, methodology, timeline, and cost estimates. Ensure they address your key objectives and provide clear plans for system configuration, data migration, integration, customisation, and training.
- Collaborate on solution design with potential partners and involve your CRM platform owner and administrator in the process. They will play crucial roles in maintaining the

solution once it's live and ensure it aligns with your business needs.
- Verify that the implementation partners offer comprehensive training and ongoing support services. Adequate training is crucial for user adoption and proficiency with any CRM tool. Additionally, enquire about their post-implementation support services, such as help desk support, system maintenance, and updates.
- Evaluate the project management approach of potential partners. A well-defined project management methodology ensures effective planning, communication, and coordination throughout the implementation process.

Remember that choosing the right implementation partner is essential, as it involves collaboration, trust, and effective communication.

Select a partner who understands your business, values your objectives, and is committed to your long-term success.

By following the principles of the MOVE methodology and by completing your product journey and detailed MOVE canvases, you will have all the tools necessary to design a CRM strategy that aligns with your business goals. This will set the foundation for continuous improvement and evolution.

Be Action-Oriented

We find that when organisations take on big, one-off implementations, progress often stalls because there are too many moving parts. Hence an evolutionary approach allows you to always be action oriented. Focus on the priorities. Deliver results fast. Don't get bogged down in the planning.

And from a platform perspective, don't let the tail wag the dog. The business defines the requirements and the priorities—not IT.

Finally, 'Keep It Super Simple' (KISS). When you're diving into CRM, there's a world of possibilities, tools, and integrations to explore. But before you get lost in the vastness, remember to KISS it. Don't make the challenge bigger than it needs to be. And match the solution to your organisation's maturity and capability.

For example, we often see customers stuck in the complexity of scoping opportunities, products, price books, quotes, orders, and contracts. Just because all these features are given to you in your CRM, it does not mean you have to use them.

Consider getting started by only implementing opportunities and a drop-down list of products before you start implementing complex features your sales team won't use.

Being action-oriented and rapidly delivering solutions on your CRM platform gets you business results fast.

User Adoption

Throughout this book, we have talked about the importance of accountability and involving the entire business in your strategy, process, and platform build. User adoption is one of the key reasons for doing this.

You may have the best implementation in the world, but if your team doesn't use it, you won't get the result you wanted.

> *An average system used well is more powerful than a state-of-the-art platform poorly adopted.*

To ensure that your team embraces and effectively uses the CRM system, here are some best practices and strategies to promote user adoption.

- **Communicate the Benefits:** Clearly articulate the advantages of using the CRM platform to the end-users. Explain how it will simplify their work, enhance efficiency, and contribute to achieving their goals. Emphasise the value it brings to their daily tasks, such as improved customer insights, streamlined processes, and increased collaboration.

- **Executive Sponsorship:** Obtain support and sponsorship from top-level executives for the CRM initiative. When employees see that management is committed to the CRM initiative, they are more likely to adopt it. Executives should actively promote and encourage the use of the CRM platform, leading by example.
- **User Involvement and Training:** Involve end-users in the CRM design and implementation process from the beginning. Seek their input and feedback to ensure that the CRM platform meets their needs and requirements. Provide comprehensive training programs tailored to different user roles and responsibilities. Make the training interactive, practical, and ongoing to reinforce learning and address any questions or concerns.
- **User-Friendly Interface:** Focus on designing a user-friendly interface. A well-designed interface reduces the learning curve and frustration, making it easier for users to embrace the system. Customise the interface to match the specific needs and preferences of your organisation and users.
- **Highlight Success Stories:** Share success stories and case studies of how the CRM platform has benefited other teams or individuals within the organisation. This helps build confidence and enthusiasm among users by demonstrating real-world examples of how the platform can positively impact their work.
- **Provide Ongoing Support:** Establish a dedicated support system for users to address their questions, issues, and feedback. This could include a help desk, online resources, user forums, or regular user group meetings. Promptly address any concerns or obstacles that your users may encounter to ensure their continued confidence in the CRM platform.
- **Monitor and Measure Adoption:** Continuously monitor user adoption rates and gather feedback on the CRM platform. Utilise analytics and reporting tools within the CRM system

to track usage, identify areas for improvement, and measure the impact of the platform on key performance indicators (KPIs). Regularly communicate these metrics to stakeholders to showcase the value and encourage further adoption.

Remember that user adoption is an ongoing process that requires consistent effort and engagement from all levels of the organisation. By implementing these strategies, you can increase the likelihood of a successful CRM platform adoption and maximise the benefits for your organisation.

CHOOSING A CRM PLATFORM

At its core, a CRM platform is a software application or a suite of applications that helps companies implement and monitor their CRM strategy.

A CRM platform is so much more than a contact management database. It provides:

- A Unified View of the Customer: One place to integrate all your customer interactions with your company, team, and products into a single view.
- Lifecycle Management: Enables the management and measurement of the customer lifecycle, helping to identify where customers are in their journey and what their next best action is.
- Business Process Automation: Systematizes and automates business processes, allowing for scalability and improvements in productivity.
- Organisational Alignment: Brings the entire organisation together in one place, aligned with business KPIs.
- Data Collection and Analysis: Facilitates the collection of customer data and access to trends and insights.
- Integration with Other Systems: Integrates with other business systems for marketing automation, analytics, communication tools, and more.

However, a CRM platform is only as good as the data you store, the processes you build, and the reports you create and review. And of course, it is important that you actually use the platform.

"Implementing a CRM system will do absolutely nothing for your business. However, the continued and effective use of it will." – Bobby Darnell, 'Time For Dervin – Living Large In Geiggityville'

One of our authors, Kristen, can back this up with an example:

In the early 2000s, I found myself working as the head of VIP for a leading international online gaming company. At that time, my responsibilities included overseeing 7,000 VIP customers from various countries and managing a team of marketers and analysts based in London—while our VIP account managers were situated in Greece.

Our existing back-office system proved inadequate, as it failed to provide crucial, concise customer data in real-time, hampering our account managers' ability to make informed decisions while engaging with our valuable clients over the phone.

Considering the high stakes involved in dealing with significant sums of money and prestigious clientele, I couldn't rely on my team to mentally calculate offers on the fly. Complicating matters further, the account managers worked in shifts, making it challenging to ensure consistent follow-up on customer issues and prioritisation of their needs. Traditional spreadsheets were ill-suited to addressing these challenges effectively.

During this time, Salesforce was still an emerging start-up. Faced with these limitations, I took it upon myself to clearly define the requirements and tasked my developer with creating a 'basic CRM platform'. This solution provided my team with summarised customer data, including the total value of each customer, with a breakdown of the past three months.

Armed with this information, our account managers could now make informed decisions in real-time, avoiding the pitfalls of guesswork and erroneously rewarding customers who voiced complaints rather than those who truly deserved it. Moreover, this capability empowered our marketing and analytics team to upload customer lists for proactive outreach, enabling personalised offers and incentives.

By measuring average response times to address inquiries, assigning customers to specific account managers, and tracking their performance in terms of regular monthly contacts, I was able to effectively manage the relationships with our most valuable customers across different countries, time zones, and functional teams.

This basic CRM platform became a catalyst for improving our planning and processes, ultimately leading to significant growth in revenue. Within just nine months, the revenue generated by these customers increased from 65% of the overall net revenue to over 72%.

It was through this experience and seeing first-hand how CRM strategies, processes, and platforms can positively impact business performance while delivering great customer outcomes, that my interest and passion for CRM grew.

Implementing a CRM platform without a clear understanding of your customer strategy and customer lifecycle can be expensive. It can lead to wasted resources and missed opportunities.

What does a CRM platform do?

A Customer Relationship Management (CRM) system allows you to collect, store, and analyse your customer data to maximise the potential of each and every customer. And they allow you to systematise how your team interacts with your customers, driving productivity and enabling you to scale.

Let's break this down:

Understanding Your Customers

To serve your customers effectively, you need to know who they are. This includes their demographics, interests, and behaviours. For businesses, relevant details include the company's size, industry, and revenue. By understanding these aspects, you can better segment your customers and tailor your approach to meet their specific needs.

Tracking Customer Activities

CRM platforms track all customer interactions, not just their purchases. By capturing your customer's product interests, purchases, and position in the marketing and sales funnels, you can better understand their preferences and accurately predict their future buying behaviour.

CRM platforms can track and manage customer interactions, from website visits to customer service inquiries, including emails, phone calls, meetings, chats, and support tickets. Leveraging this information allows your team to provide consistent and personalised communication, ensuring exceptional customer experiences.

Systemising Processes

Once you have all your customer data, a CRM helps systemise your marketing, sales, support, and delivery processes. This streamlines operations and provides consistent service and delivery ensuring that every customer is guided smoothly through their journey with you, from initial contact to post-sale support.

Do You Need a CRM Platform?

If you're having trouble keeping track of customer information or finding it challenging to monitor your sales team's performance, a CRM platform could be the solution.

Here are some common signs that indicate you might benefit from a CRM platform:

- Difficulty in Tracking Customer and Sales Information: If you struggle to keep track of customer details, interactions, and sales activities, a CRM platform can centralise this information for easy access and management.
- Inconsistent Follow-Up on Tasks Related to Prospects and Customers: A CRM platform helps automate reminders and follow-ups, ensuring no opportunities fall through the cracks.
- Overwhelmed Team Members Who are Constantly Busy: With a CRM platform, repetitive tasks can be automated, freeing up your team to focus on high-value activities.
- Managing Work Through Multiple Spreadsheets: A CRM platform consolidates data from various sources, eliminating the need for cumbersome spreadsheets and improving data accuracy.
- Need For Better Coordination of Sales and Marketing Efforts: A CRM platform aligns sales and marketing activities, ensuring a seamless customer journey from lead to sale.
- Concerns About Losing Valuable Knowledge When Staff Members Leave: A CRM platform retains all customer interactions and information, safeguarding against the loss of valuable data when employees depart.

What Features Do You Need?

We have categorised the core features you may need in a CRM platform to help you better understand and assess the features and functionality when choosing a platform for your business.

When choosing a CRM, there are four core areas to focus on:

- Your **customers** and their profile (or identity), their transactions and their interactions with you.
- Your **team**, how they work with your customers, how you manage and incentivise them, and how they work together.
- The **platform** and the tools and technology that they provide.

- The software **vendor** and how established they are, the support they give, and the ecosystem of partners, consultants, and implementers.

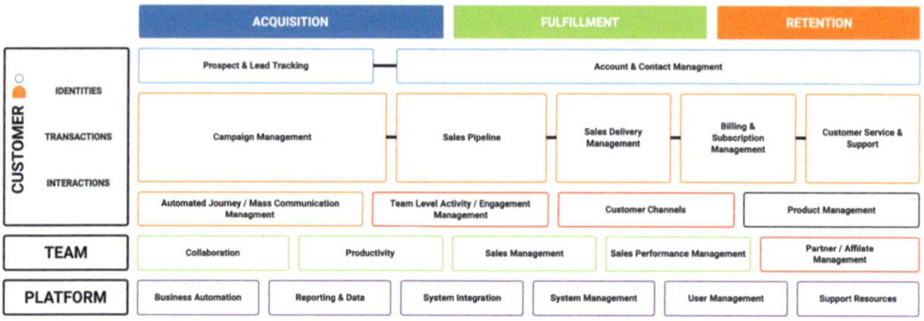

Components of CRM Functionality

The Ultimate Statement of Requirements Checklist

When you're ready to choose a CRM platform, it's important to list out everything you need. We have created a detailed checklist of items to help you make sure you don't miss anything important.

Your Customers

Prospect and Leads Tracking:

Capture and qualify leads from various sources such as web forms, social media, and email campaigns.

- **Lead Capture** (web, email, etc.): Gather leads from sources like web forms and emails.
- **Prospects:** Keep records of new potential customers from first contact to conversion.
- **Lead Scoring:** Prioritise leads based on how much they interact with you (e.g. web visits, email opens).
- **Activity Tracking:** Track emails and calls.
- **Integration with Marketing Automation Platform:** Connect with marketing tools like email and social media marketing platforms to maintain engagement.
- **Social Media Capture:** Collect leads directly from integration with social media platforms.

Account and Contact Management

Centralise customer records to keep all customer information in one place. Avoid duplicates to maintain data accuracy and consistency.

- **Account Management:** Manage customers at an account level, not contact level. Especially important if you are a B2B business.
- **Contact Management:** Keep detailed records of all customer contacts and their profile information.
- **Subscription Management:** Let customers opt in or out of communication channels.
- **Preference Centre:** Let customers choose what they want to receive from you.
- **Social Media Integration:** Include social media details (e.g. LinkedIn) to better know your customers.
- **Survey:** Use surveys to get customer feedback (for example Net Promoter Scores).
- **Loyalty Programs:** Manage programs to reward repeat customers.
- **Updating Contact Information:** Allow customers to keep their own contact details up to date.

Your CRM Processes

Campaign Management

Create and manage lists for targeted marketing campaigns. Measure which campaigns can be attributed to sales. Monitor budget and revenue to measure ROI.

- **Campaign List Generation:** Create contact lists for specific marketing campaigns and track which campaign members engage with each campaign.
- **Engage with Campaign Members:** The ability to email, call, or engage with campaign members
- **Campaign Attribution:** Attribute opportunities to campaigns and measure campaign influence.
- **Budget and Revenue Tracking:** Monitor campaign costs and returns.

Sales Pipeline:

Track sales opportunities from initial contact to closing the deal. Manage sales processes to streamline operations. Predict revenue to help with planning and forecasting.

- **Opportunity Management:** Track sales opportunities from start to finish.
- **Opportunity Scoring:** Score opportunities to prioritise them.
- **Pipeline Management:** Manage the sales pipeline in real time.
- **List Generation:** Create lists for sales activities.
- **Sales Process Scripts:** Provide scripts for sales processes.
- **Sales Activity Management:** Track all sales activities.

Sales Delivery

Manage quotes, orders, and contracts efficiently. Handle billing and subscriptions smoothly. Integrate with e-commerce platforms for seamless sales processes.

- **Proposal Management:** Create and manage sales proposals.
- **Quote and Order Management:** Handle quotes and orders accurately.
- **Contracts:** Manage customer contracts.
- **Billing and Subscription:** Process billing and manage subscriptions.
- **Integration with Website/Shopping Carts:** Connect with e-commerce platforms.
- **Customer Self-Service Access to Sales Orders:** Let customers view their sales orders.

Billing and Subscription Management

Handle all aspects of billing, including payment processing, credits, and refunds. Integrate with accounting systems for smooth financial management. Support multi-company, currency, and language operations for global reach.

- **Payment Links and Processing:** Provide secure payment options.

- **Accounting System Integration:** Connect with accounting software.
- **Billing Invoices and Payment:** Manage invoices and payments.
- **Credits and Refunds:** Process credits and refunds quickly.
- **Debtor Status:** Track outstanding payments.
- **Multi-Company, Currency, and Lingual Capability:** Support global operations.

Service and Support

Create and resolve customer issues efficiently through case management. Provide a customer support portal for self-service. Maintain a knowledge base for common issues and solutions. Manage service levels and field services to ensure customer satisfaction.

- **Case Management:** Track and manage customer support cases.
- **Customer Support Portal:** Let customers access support resources.
- **Knowledge Base:** Keep a database of support articles.
- **Call Centre and Logging:** Manage call centre operations and logs.
- **Ticket Escalation:** Automatically escalate support tickets.
- **Field Service Management:** Manage field service operations.
- **Service Level Agreement Management:** Track and manage SLAs.

Product Management

Configure and manage product information, including pricing. Support cross-selling and up-selling strategies. Ensure timely product delivery and manage returns.

- **Product Configuration:** Configure product details.
- **Prices:** Manage product pricing.
- **Cross-Selling and Up-Selling:** Encourage additional purchases.

- **Delivery:** Coordinate product delivery.
- **Website Product Catalogue:** Keep an online product catalogue.
- **Customer Returns/RMA:** Manage returns efficiently.
- **Fulfilling Orders:** Ensure orders are fulfilled on time.
- **Customer Portal:** Provide a portal for customers to manage their accounts.

Activity Tracking

Track all tasks, meetings, and communications. Integrate with calendars and email clients for seamless scheduling. Log call details to maintain a complete interaction history.

- **Task and Activity Tracking:** Keep track of tasks and activities.
- **Meeting Scheduling:** Schedule and manage meetings.
- **Calendar:** Integrate with calendar systems.
- **Email Client Integrations:** Connect with email clients.
- **Call Dialling:** Make calls directly from the CRM.
- **Call Logging:** Log call details.

Customer Channels

Provide customer portals for self-service and account management. Enable customers to access information and manage their accounts easily.

- **Customer Portal:** Provide a portal for customers to interact with your business.
- **Omnichannel:** Support multiple communication channels. (WhatsApp, Chatbot)

Managing Your Team

Sales Management

Support your sales team with territory and quota management, performance tracking, incentive and compensation management, and sales forecasting to aid strategic planning.

- **Territory and Quota Management:** Manage sales territories and quotas.
- **Forecasting:** Predict sales outcomes.
- **Performance Tracking:** Monitor sales performance.
- **Account Management:** Manage customer accounts.
- **Incentive and Compensation Management:** Handle sales incentives and compensation.

Sales Performance

Monitoring sales targets, managing incentives and commissions, using gamification to engage the sales team, supporting team-based selling, and managing relationships with sales partners

- **Sales Target Tracking:** Track sales targets.
- **Sales Incentives and Commissions:** Manage sales incentives and commissions.
- **Gamification:** Use games to motivate the sales team.
- **Team Selling:** Facilitate team-based selling.
- **Sales Partner Management:** Manage relationships with sales partners.

Productivity

Enhance productivity with personalised tools and document management. Provide web and mobile access to ensure your team can work from anywhere.

- **Personalisation:** Customise the CRM for each user.
- **Document and Content Management:** Manage documents and content easily.
- **Web Access:** Ensure easy web access from anywhere.
- **Mobile Access:** Provide mobile access for on-the-go management.

Collaboration

Improve communication and teamwork with tagging, comments, and feeds. Provide real-time notifications to keep everyone informed. Manage user profiles for better collaboration.

- **Record Tagging, Comments, and Feeds:** Enhance teamwork with tagging and commenting.
- **Notifications:** Provide real-time notifications for important events.
- **User Profiles:** Manage detailed user profiles.

The CRM Platform

Reporting and Data

Generate detailed reports and customisable dashboards. Ensure data security and compliance with data protection regulations. Provide tools for data import, export, and integration with other systems.

- **Reporting:** Generate detailed and customisable reports.
- **Dashboards:** Create dynamic dashboards for data visualisation.
- **Customer Reporting:** Provide tailored customer-specific reports.
- **Data Import and Export Tools:** Facilitate easy data import and export.
- **Integration APIs:** Ensure seamless integration with other systems.
- **Security of Data:** Implement strong data security measures.
- **Access and Ownership of Data:** Manage data access and ownership.
- **Backup and Recovery:** Ensure data backup and recovery.

User Management

Manage user roles and access to ensure data protection. Provide secure access to sensitive information. Control access at the account and field levels.

- **User, Role, and Access Management:** Manage user roles and access levels.
- **Object, Record, and Field Level Protection:** Protect data at various levels.
- **Account Level Access:** Control access to accounts.
- **Secure Access:** Provide secure access to the CRM.

Business Automation

Automate workflows and approval processes to streamline operations. Create custom objects and fields to tailor the CRM to your needs. Enable no-code process building for easy customisation.

- **Custom Objects and Fields:** Create and manage custom objects and fields.
- **Workflow and Approvals:** Automate workflows and approval processes.
- **No-Code Process Building/Journey:** Enable no-code process building.
- **Application Development:** Support custom development with technical code.

System Management

Provide sandbox and test environments for safe testing. Monitor system performance to ensure reliability. Manage data volumes and maintain high data quality.

- **Sandbox/Test Environments:** Provide sandbox and test environments.
- **Performance Management:** Monitor and manage system performance.
- **System Performance:** Ensure the CRM performs well under various loads.
- **Data Volumes and Quality:** Manage large data volumes and maintain high data quality.
- **Reliability:** Ensure the system is reliable and robust.

The Software Vendor

Vendor Reputation:

- **Reputation:** How long has the company been in business and what reputation does it have in the market?
- **Support and Training:** Ensure the vendor provides good customer support and training resources.
- **Breadth of Partner Applications:** Evaluate the availability of third-party add-ons or plugins.

- **Updates and Upgrades:** Check how often the vendor updates and upgrades the system.
- **Vendor Roadmap:** Look at the vendor's future plans for features and enhancements.
- **Community and Ecosystem:** Ensure there is an active user community and support.

Implementation

What is the level of effort and support required to implement the platform

- **Assistance with Setup:** Get help with setting up and configuring the CRM.
- **Cost:** Consider the total cost of ownership, including subscription fees, implementation costs, and extra charges.
- **Deployment Options:** Decide between cloud-based or on-premises solutions.
- **Data Migration:** Ensure ease of migrating existing data to the new system.
- **Availability of Skills and Resources:** Make sure your team has the necessary skills and resources.

The Final Decision – Which CRM?

If you have not already done so, it's essential to go through the process of the MOVE methodology to map your customer journeys, define ownership, understand your data, know what metrics you need visibility on, and finally to understand your internal capability (covered under 'E for Evolution').

Understanding Your Business Needs

These should be very clear to you now that you have mapped your customer journeys:

- What are your primary business objectives?
- What specific problems are you trying to solve with a CRM platform?

- Which departments will be using the CRM platform?
- What features are essential for your business operations?

Assessing Your Technical Capabilities

Evaluate your organisation's technical capabilities:

- What is your current IT infrastructure?
- Do you have in-house IT support?
- Are you looking for a cloud-based or on-premises solution?
- How tech-savvy are your employees?

Understanding your technical landscape will help you narrow down CRM options that are compatible with your existing systems and user capabilities.

Defining Your Budget

CRM costs can vary widely, so it's essential to establish a realistic budget. Consider:

- Initial licensing or subscription fees
- Implementation costs
- Training expenses
- Ongoing maintenance and support costs
- Potential customisation or integration expenses

Remember, the cheapest option isn't always the most cost-effective in the long run. Focus on value rather than just price.

Researching CRM Options

- With your requirements, capabilities, and budget in mind, start researching CRM options
- Read industry reports and reviews
- Ask for recommendations from peers in your industry
- Explore case studies of businesses similar to yours
- Create a shortlist of potential CRM vendors

Evaluate Key Features

Use the comprehensive checklist we have provided to list all the features you will need.

Rank and prioritise the must have, should have, could have, or want to have features you need.

Some features may not be critical at the start of the implementation, but as you evolve, they will be. Make sure you consider them upfront. For example, your immediate problem may be to solve your sales management problem. After that, you will need to introduce a service and support solution.

Requesting Demos and Trials

Once you've narrowed down your options, request demos or free trials from your top choices. This hands-on experience will give you valuable insights into:

- User interface and ease of use
- Functionality and feature set
- Customisation capabilities
- Integration with your existing tools
- Customer support quality

Involve key stakeholders in this process to gather diverse perspectives.

Considering Implementation and Training

A CRM is only as good as its implementation and user adoption. Consider:

- The vendor's implementation process and timeline
- Available training resources
- Ongoing support options
- User adoption strategies

Making the Final Decision

After thorough evaluation, it's now time to make your decision. Consider:

- How well the CRM meets your defined requirements
- Total cost of ownership
- Scalability for future growth
- User feedback from trials or demos
- Vendor reputation and stability

Remember, choosing a CRM is a significant decision that can impact your business for years to come. Take your time, involve key stakeholders, and make an informed choice based on your unique business needs and goals.

By following this structured approach, you'll be well-equipped to select a CRM platform that not only meets your current needs but also supports your business growth in the long term.

THANK YOU

We sincerely hope you found this book useful and we thank you for taking the time to read it.

We are on a mission to demystify CRM. So, if this book helped you, we would really appreciate you telling others by leaving a helpful review.

Please visit: moveyourcustomer.com/review

FREE RESOURCE CENTRE

Scan to access your free resource hub that includes bonus content, videos, templates, and articles.

https://link.moveyourcustomer.com/tmm

Made in United States
Cleveland, OH
05 November 2026

47601849R00083